LEGEND
of the
GOLDEN
SCROLLS

How to Order:
Single copies may be ordered from Prima Publishing, P.O. Box 1260BK, Rocklin, CA 95677; telephone (916) 632-4400. Quantity discounts are also available. On your letterhead, include information concerning the intended use of the books and the number of books you wish to purchase.

—ᴍ—

LEGEND
of the
GOLDEN
SCROLLS

Ageless Secrets for Building Wealth

—ᴍ—

GLENN BLAND

PRIMA PUBLISHING

© 1995 by Glenn Bland

Cover design by Linda Dunlavey, The Dunlavey Studio, Inc.
Cover illustration © 1994, Greg Spalenka

Library of Congress Cataloging-in-Publication Data
Bland, Glenn.
    Legend of the golden scrolls: ageless secrets for building
    wealth / Glenn Bland.
       p. cm.
    Includes index.
    ISBN 1-55958-705-9
    1. Conduct of life. 2. Money—Moral and ethical aspects.
3. Peace of mind. 4. Worldliness. I. Title.
BJ1581.2.B55   1995
158'.1—dc20   94-38998
                                                        CIP

96 97 98 99 AA 10 9 8 7 6 5 4 3 2
Printed in the United States of America

*To Leesa, Keith, and Joey—
lights in darkness.*

CONTENTS

—∿—

ACKNOWLEDGMENTS

To Deborah Huff, Larry Jensen, Amy Bland, and Verna Beth Bland for their assistance. To Charles Henry for being sensitive to the heart of a writer and for being a genuine friend.

PREFACE

Proof positive that the essence of wealth is indeed mysterious is revealed through the reality that so few people possess it. Those few on whom good fortune smiles, either knowingly or unknowingly, follow certain precepts that unlock the mystery and bring financial rewards. You too may join the elite ranks of these wealth builders by grasping and practicing the same precepts that are unveiled herein.

Money is the master of the uninformed but the bondslave of the enlightened. Money has been instrumental in both the rise and fall of nations and kings. It affects every area of life for both common and uncommon men. There is no earthly escape from its power and influence. Money knows no worldly equivalent, yet so little is known of its real essence. This is the truth of the matter today as well as throughout the eternal landscape of the past.

Since money has such a predominant impact on every man, woman, and child living on this celestial globe, every person should understand it. No human being should live in need of it. This book was written for that paramount purpose.

For more than three decades, I have counseled hundreds of people regarding their personal finances. Although most of them were well educated by modern standards, I have found the majority lacking instruction in financial matters. Consequently, many have experienced financial failure even though their incomes were more than adequate. This publication grew from my involvement with these people.

PREFACE

I have used *he, his,* and *him* to refer to both the masculine and feminine genders throughout this book. This was done solely to facilitate the writing. Fortunately, the principles of financial success are gender neutral. They remain suspended in time awaiting the hour when you will summon them to serve you and make you rich.

G.D.B.
Memphis, Tennessee

LEGEND

of the

GOLDEN
SCROLLS

I

———

*Enduring wealth comes
to no man until he
prepares himself
to receive it.*

———

FINANCIAL
AWAKENING

—〰—

Eighty-nine years before the 1947 discovery of the celebrated Dead Sea Scrolls at Qumran, a similar but different treasure was uncovered in that changeless region at Murabba'at. From the fabled account of this earliest find, *Legend of the Golden Scrolls* originated and grew. The legend continues to be rekindled because everyone who follows its wisdom prospers prodigiously.

The tale began with a young Bedouin man of the Ta'amireh tribe named Akkash. He was extremely tall for an Arab, raw boned and dark skinned—the genuine product of a Spartan desert life. His face revealed the harsh evidence of endless days of exposure to the incessant winds and scorching sun. His long, straight, Semitic nose was framed by a curly raven beard and accented by his smoldering ebony eyes. His wavy pitch-black hair fell wildly around his ears and flowed down the nape of his neck to his shoulders. Akkash, in every sense, was a true son of the wilderness of Judah.

From early boyhood, Akkash lived the solitary life of a shepherd, returning to the Ta'amireh camp only when his meager provisions ran out. He knew how to live off of the land, even the forbidden land of the Judean wilderness; without exception, it is the

3

wildest and most desolate place in the Middle East. Yet, the sheep and goats of Akkash were plump and healthy and brought top prices at the market in Bethlehem. Trained in desert lore and survival at his father's knee, he knew how to care for his herd even under the most intractable circumstances.

Akkash followed his sheep and goats as they slowly grazed the rock strewn gullies of the Wady Darajeh toward the Dead Sea. He used his long staff to clear a footpath on which to walk. Narrow ravines branched off of the wady in every direction, turning into deep gorges. Thin ridges of dark brown limestone, capped with gleaming white chalk, stood majestic against the azure sky that surrounded him. His thoughts wandered to a distant past when his ancestors had pastured their flocks in the very place he gazed upon.

Moments passed before he regained his presence of mind. All at once he discovered that one of his goats had strayed from the herd. Akkash called the animal, to no avail. He said to himself, "Dumb goat!" and wearily set out to return the wandering animal to the herd. The goat climbed the craggy rocks of a limestone cliff higher and higher as the shepherd followed, calling to it each step of the way. The sun beat upon him mercilessly. His breath came in short gasps. The muscles in his legs became weakened. He desperately needed rest.

Akkash reached a small ledge in the shade of an overhanging rock. He wet his parched throat with a drink from his goatskin. He sat back against the face of the cliff, stretched out his legs, and relaxed. The young shepherd had the eyes of an eagle and he began to survey the panoramic view before him. From the great cliff where he sat, the landscape descended some 2,000 feet to the stone covered shoreline of the Dead Sea. He gazed at the placid shining waters of salt blue. A rare solitude indeed.

The stillness of the moment was overwhelming. No sound of reeds stirred in the wind. No rustle of leaves blew in the breeze. No babbling water flowed through rocky shoals. No sound of life at all, except for a single jackal's wail that echoed through lonely gorges.

Akkash searched the craggy rocks above for a sign of his wandering goat. His eyes covered the higher elevation inch by inch. For some unexplainable reason, they came to rest on a mysterious hole, no larger than the wheel of a goat cart, that was little more than 20 feet above the place he sat. The hole piqued his curiosity because it appeared to go somewhere. It might lead to something such as a cave, yet the opening was much too high and too small to be a typical cave entrance, of which there were many in the area.

Akkash got to his feet, took a smooth round stone from the sheepskin satchel hooked to his belt, and placed it in the leather of his slingshot. He whirled the slingshot around his head twice, and then on the third spin let the stone fly in the direction of the hole. It found its mark, entering the opening directly through its center. The young shepherd heard the crack of the missile hitting an inner stone wall and then the undeniable clank of rock against pottery, as the missile bounded to the floor of the chamber. The "clank" was undeniable to him because he had used old clay jars for target practice many times during his childhood.

Upon hearing the sound, Akkash's heart began to pound and his ears perked. He took another round stone, sailed it through the opening, and listened. Again, he heard the familiar clank. He then became somewhat frightened, thinking he might have encroached on a jinn abode, where a desert spirit dwelled. His first inclination was to run and distance himself from this place, but his youthful curiosity outweighed his fear and he decided that he must take a peek into the hole above.

With some measure of fear and trepidation, the Bedouin climbed the vertical face of the cliff. His hands reached the opening, which he grasped, and he pulled himself up so that he could peer inside where the light was faint. As his eyes became adjusted to the darkness of the inner chamber, he saw images of a dozen or so large clay jars in a cave that measured no more than fifteen feet from wall to wall. Sections of the rock ceiling had broken away sometime in the distant past and crashed on top of several jars, smashing them into small pieces.

The opening was just large enough for a man to squeeze through. The shepherd's fear subsided upon discovering the cave uninhabited either by man or spirit. He crawled through the hole and dropped approximately 6 feet to the cave's floor. He counted the jars that remained unbroken. There were thirteen: seven of them were about 2 feet tall and six measured nearly 3 feet. They were all cylindrical, having wide necks and large bowl-like lids. Akkash's imagination began to envision jars full of ancient jewels and gold. He would be rich!

The Bedouin lifted the lid of one of the larger jars and turned it upside down. A single old sandal tumbled out. Then he checked another, and another, until all of the larger jars were emptied. The only treasure he found consisted of relics from the past: cloth so brittle that it flaked apart, three deteriorated leather sandals, and a small tarnished brass lamp. Akkash's momentary dream of riches suddenly transformed into a state of utter disappointment.

In his growing despair, he then picked up a small clay jar and poured its contents on the floor. A leather cylinder lay before him, with strange writing imprinted on it. A leather cap covered one end. He picked up the cylinder and with some difficulty removed the cap to see something rolled up and stuffed into the container. He attempted to remove the object, but it was brittle and stuck to the leather cylinder. The Bedouin replaced the cap over the end and gently laid the container on a shelf of rock that protruded from the cave's wall.

Akkash then removed the lid of another small clay jar and turned it bottom-up; again a leather cylinder toppled to the floor. He let it lie where it had fallen and opened another jar, then another, and another, until six identical containers lay at his feet. Next, he scanned the cave for anything he might have missed. There was nothing, except an ancient wooden adze handle, which still had the leather bindings that secured the attached flint blade. The shepherd mumbled to himself, "Worthless . . . nothing but old rubbish."

The cave was hot and musty. Perspiration trickled down Akkash's forehead and stung his eyes. He wiped his brow with his sleeve, picked up the six leather cylinders, and reached for the seventh on the rock shelf. He put each of them through the hole and one by one they dropped to the ledge below. Then he pulled himself up, squeezed out of the opening into the sunshine and fresh air, and plummeted on top of the seven containers. Slowly getting to his feet, he dusted the dirt from his clothing. His stray goat now stood before him having an expression of sheer surprise. The Bedouin shouted angrily, "Dumb goat! Crazy goat! You are the cause of this!" and tossed a stone at the nanny, who immediately bounded off the ledge and ran back to the herd.

Akkash carried the seven leather cylinders down the cliff like an arm-load of firewood. He returned to his grazing flock, keeping his eyes on the mischievous black and white goat. The nanny nonchalantly nipped a sprig of grass here and there, paying little notice to her irritated keeper. Once more he thought, "Dumb goat."

The shepherd selected a small boulder located in the midst of his herd and sat down to inspect the queer looking objects. As the sun lowered over the western horizon, there was enough light to examine each item. He determined that the seven cylinders had the very same external markings. The writing imprinted in the leather was completely foreign. Although he could remove the end caps from two of the containers, he could not remove their contents. The deterioration of the material over what he assumed to be centuries had stuck them together with a glue-like substance. Akkash's better judgment told him to put the cylinders away and keep them for another day.

The Bedouin kept the seven mysterious leather containers with him over the next two years. He revealed only to his father that he had them. The elder Bedouin had seen many relics. Rarely had any of them been of real value, so he paid little interest to

Akkash's find. However, the young Bedouin became attached to his relics and hoped to find someone to interpret the odd writing on the containers.

During those years the leather cylinders were stashed in Akkash's wool knapsack. They weathered extreme heat, fierce cold, cloudbursts, sandstorms, and a dangerous bout with a hostile band of desert riffraff. In each instance, Akkash protected his relics like priceless treasures. Why? Because they were something that he alone owned and his affection for them continually grew stronger. At times, while sitting alone by his campfire, he would take the seven containers from his knapsack, place them on the sand in the firelight, and simply look at them, wishing they could tell him of their esoteric past.

One delightful spring day, the shepherd followed his flock in search of pasture along the Wady Qumran, a seasonal river that empties into the Dead Sea. As his herd approached the shore, Akkash saw a young man, who was obviously American, staring out over the briny blue water.

The shepherd observed the foreigner with growing curiosity. The American playfully skipped flat rocks across the placid surface of the sea. Several of them skipped more than 10 times before slowly sinking to the bottom. Akkash thought about the many times he had played that game.

When the herd had grazed within earshot, the foreigner suddenly turned and faced Akkash, revealing an expression of unmitigated surprise at discovering he was not alone. He quickly regained his composure, took his wide brimmed hat in his hand, put it above his head, and made a friendly waving gesture. The Bedouin was pleased and lifted his staff in a reciprocal manner.

Akkash made his camp a stone's throw from the rocky shoreline and within sight of the American. However, he paid him no attention, as he gathered his flock into a small gully where the animals could bed down for the onrushing night. The shepherd built a fire from twigs and driftwood, as the dusk quickly faded into darkness. He held his hands over the flames, as his eyes searched the darkness surrounding him. They halted momentarily on the red glow that pierced the night from the foreigner's camp. He mumbled, "The American must be warming himself also."

The hour was yet early, but fatigue gripped the shepherd's body. He lay back using his folded knapsack for a pillow and closed his eyes. A deep slumber quickly ensued.

The crunch of footsteps upon the sandy pea gravel where he slept awakened Akkash with a start. His eyes sprung open to discover a man standing over him. In the dim firelight, he recognized the American. To his surprise, the foreigner held a little white lamb in his arms. The Bedouin wiped the sleep from his eyes as he abruptly sat up.

"Friend," the American said, "this lamb strayed into my camp and I am returning it to its mother." Akkash understood English, so he gave his approval with a wide smile and a nod. The foreigner carried the lamb amidst the flock and gently put it down. Its mother found it immediately and nestled it with her nose. The American stepped back to observe, obviously amused and pleased.

When the foreigner returned to the firelight, the Bedouin stood and made a low graceful bow and said, "May Allah be your keeper. My name is Akkash. How can I repay you for the kind act you have showed me? I am in your debt."

"My name is Andy and you owe me nothing," the young American replied.

"Then you must honor me with your presence to partake of bread and Ta'amireh wine, so that your sleep under the desert stars will be peaceful and deep," Akkash countered.

Andy thought for a moment, then nodded. The shepherd made a gesture for him to be seated on a black wool blanket next to the fire. Akkash sat beside him and passed him unleavened bread and a small goatskin filled with rich red wine. Andy tore the bread apart with his teeth and chewed his tasteless, coarse mouthful until his jaws tired. Then he swallowed. He quickly chased the bread down with two generous drinks of wine, which he found heavy and harsh. He wondered how the Bedouin could live on such comestibles as this.

"I must repay you for returning the lamb, for it is the law of my fathers," Akkash said through a sloshing mouthful of bread and wine. "If I do not repay you, Allah will be displeased with me and something bad will happen to me or my herd."

As he listened, Andy realized that he must agree or else violate an ancient custom of Akkash's people, which would be a disgrace in the eyes of the Bedouin. So he nodded just before taking another bite of the tough bread.

The shepherd asked, "Where do you come from in America?"

"Pennsylvania," the foreigner answered as he took another drink of wine.

"What brings you to this remote land of scarcity?"

"I'm looking for some answers. This is the land where David, John the Baptist, and Jesus found purpose and meaning. I reasoned that if it worked for them, it would also work for me. So, here I am."

"What answers do you seek here?"

"I'm now in my twenties and I've been a bobbin boy in a cotton factory, a telegraph messenger, and telegraph operator. I've not yet discovered my life's calling and I've always been poor. So, that's what I'm looking for—my purpose in life and how to escape the slavery of poverty. Something told me I could find those answers here. I withdrew my skimpy savings from the bank, purchased boat passage, and came to this wilderness. This is my fourth day here and I have found no answers thus far, but I'm still optimistic."

Instant rapport developed between the two young men. Akkash, who had always been satisfied with his Spartan existence, did not comprehend everything that his new friend said, but still, he empathized with him.

"How can I help you find these . . . these . . . answers?" the Bedouin asked.

"There is nothing you can do," the foreigner answered. "For the quest is something that I alone must pursue."

"Huh," Akkash responded. "I do not understand you Americans. You talk very strange."

"Well," Andy said, "I should return to my camp now and turn in for the night. Thank you very much for sharing your bread and wine with me." He then rose to his feet.

"Wait!" the Bedouin called. "Before you go, it would give me much pleasure if you would accept my only possession in the world as my gift to repay you for your act of kindness."

"That's not necessary," said Andy.

"Oh, but it is," Akkash assured him as he dug through all of his belongings in the knapsack. He reached the bottom and took out the seven leather cylinders and laid them on the blanket before his new friend.

"I found these two years ago in a cave not very far from where we sit at this moment. They are very old . . . and real leather . . . see! They are now yours, with the blessing of Allah."

Andy showed immediate interest in the objects. He picked one up and turned it in his hand as he stared at the strange writing imprinted in the leather. He then reached for the other six and inspected them one by one with a keen eye, before placing them back on the blanket. He began to suspect that the leather cylinders just might have some archaeological value.

"Take them," the shepherd said. "They are my only possession; take them now." He picked them up and put them at the feet of the foreigner.

"I will receive them only if you will accept this gift from me in return."

He reached into his jacket pocket and removed a gold watch on a chain. He picked up the Bedouin's hand and placed the beautiful timepiece in his palm. He felt a sudden emptiness inside because the watch had belonged to his father.

The shepherd's eyes brightened and a broad smile spread across his face. "Yes! Yes, I will accept this for it is a thing of beauty. Thank you, my American friend," Akkash said. "Sit, and let me tell you the story of how I discovered the leather cylinders."

The foreigner again sat down by the fire and placed the seven objects in his lap. Akkash promptly began his tale, "One day I was tending my flock in the Wady Darajeh. . . ."

When Akkash finished, Andy's curiosity had piqued. Inside, he knew that something of genuine archaeological value lay in his lap. It was getting late, so he thanked Akkash, excused himself, and made his way back to his camp under the moonlit desert sky.

"Tomorrow," the Bedouin said as he walked away.

The young American's fire burned low, but the remaining coals were still red hot. He put some small twigs on the coals and fanned them with his hat until they burst into yellow-red flames. Andy sat down in the opening of his tent and gazed into the flames for an instant before refocusing his attention on the seven leather cylinders that lay on the ground in front of him. He asked himself, "What could these old relics be?" He attempted to remove the caps covering the ends of four of them before discovering the two that Akkash had loosened. He looked into the cylinders at the circular folds of both and did his best to remove their contents, but he found them immovable. Not wanting to damage them, he decided to replace their leather caps and be patient until he could seek some expert assistance.

He wearily lay back on his bedroll and thought about his father's gold watch, for it had great sentimental value. As he drifted into tranquil slumber, he thought, "I wonder if the shepherd can even tell time. . . ."

The sun rose over the hazy horizon like a giant yellow hot-air balloon ascending into the heavens. The long mountain shadows dwindled into nothingness, as the wilderness awakened under the warmth of the bright rays. The young American endeavored to open his eyes, as he tussled on his ruffled pallet to escape the unconscious effect of twilight sleep. The unfamiliar baaing of sheep searching for food brought him to his senses. His stiff body stretched as he got to his feet outside his tent. Akkash had already gathered his flock and headed them toward higher ground.

The shepherd saw Andy and waved in a sweeping motion. "Come again my friend! And may the good fortune of Allah be with you."

"I shall!" Andy yelled in return. He watched Akkash drive his herd over the rough terrain and disappear into a narrow mountain pass. Alone again, his thoughts reverted to his purpose for being there—seeking and finding answers concerning the future course of his life.

He built a fire and partook of a meager breakfast of black coffee, dried figs, and cornmeal mush. Then he packed his provisions and gear into a large brown canvas backpack, hoisted it over his shoulders, and headed west, deeper into the Judean wilderness. Every step he made was difficult. As he walked he recalled childhood stories of how this desolate land looked—as if it had been cursed and burned by fire. He believed this to be an apt description.

At the end of a two-day journey, the square-jawed American found himself in the heart of the wilderness of En-gedi, which was the place where David had sought refuge in his desperate flight from the wrath of King Saul. En-gedi was the only oasis to the west of the Dead Sea. He pulled a crude map from his hip pocket and confirmed his position. Water was plentiful. Lush vegetation grew abundantly. Wild goats roamed throughout the steep, craggy cliffs. He made camp near a clear spring partly sheltered by an overhanging slab of rock protruding nearly a dozen feet from the side of a bluff. Here he had some protection from the uncertain elements.

Determined, Andy remained at En-gedi for 20 days, all the while eagerly searching for the secrets of skillful living and financial success. As his provisions grew sparse, he learned how to fend for himself. Figs, dates, wild onions, wild oats, wild goats, and wild fowl were bounteous.

While in self-imposed isolation, he discovered much about himself that he had not known. His character and resolve were tested. All of his strengths and weaknesses surfaced. He struggled against negativism and debilitating fear. Sometimes his thoughts gave way to bizarre imaginings. His quest to "know thyself" revealed both the best and worst in him.

During the numerous occasions when he almost acknowledged defeat, he found the need to pray. When he prayed, his burdens seemed to lighten and inner peace sustained him. Sometimes unfamiliar voices penetrated his mind, befuddling him with deranged thoughts. He persistently searched within for the answers he so desperately sought, but they continued to elude him. He wondered why so many others found their way in the wilderness, yet he had not.

When his provisions finally ran out, he was exhausted, haggard, and thoroughly discouraged. With disgust, he packed his gear and bid the oasis of En-gedi goodbye. Feelings of failure overwhelmed him. With only a few dollars in his pocket, he spent two nights at the seaport of Joppa, eating little and sleeping on the docks while awaiting passage back to New York. The crossing was lengthy and uneventful.

Immediately after the steamer docked in the New York harbor, Andy had to find food and shelter, but with no money left in his pocket, where could he go? Someone recommended a Roman Catholic church just two blocks from the pier. Andy went there and asked for food and shelter. During his short stay at the church an old priest befriended him.

Andy shared his secret gift with the priest and asked if he knew what the unfamiliar writing said. No, he didn't, but after seeing the leather cylinders, the priest advised Andy to take them to the International Society of Hebrew Studies located only a few blocks away.

Learning that Andy was seeking answers to finding the abundant life, the cleric realized that his guest's views were very materialistic and without much substance. The wise priest knew that even if the young man found what he was searching for, he would still not have found the biggest prize of all—happiness and fulfillment.

That evening, after supper, the clergyman told Andy of God's everlasting love for him and how God came to earth and dwelled among men through the person of his son, Jesus. The old priest explained how it was possible for him to have an eternal relationship with God by following the teachings of His son and believing in Him. The cleric said, "My friend, wisdom dictates that if you seek the kingdom of God first, you shall then find the abundant life and all of its riches. Only then will the way be opened for you to attain the ultimate dimension of human existence."

The young man listened intensely. The things he heard made sense, for he was very aware of the spiritual vacuum in his life. Therefore, he believed.

The next morning, he reflected on the happenings of the previous evening as he sipped his black coffee in between bites of egg, bacon, and buttered toast. He felt good inside.

With the cleric's written directions in hand, the young man threw his backpack over his shoulders and walked briskly to the building on West 18th Street that housed the International Society of Hebrew Studies. It was just before nine o'clock and the reception room was empty. He rang a small service bell that sat on the reception desk and took a seat in an uncomfortable chair next to the entrance.

Within minutes, a rabbi emerged from a rear door. He was almost as round as he was tall. He had an inordinately bushy gray beard, from the midst of which a wide smile filled his face. He bowed quickly and said, "Shalom Aleichem." Somewhat surprised, the young man hastily got to his feet and feigned a bow, but said nothing.

"I am Rabbi Abraham Heschel. May I help you?"

"Yes," the young man shyly responded. "I'm Andy. I came across some interesting old relics while on a recent trip into the

Judean wilderness. They could be of Hebrew origin and I am curious to know if in fact they are."

The rabbi's eyes brightened and his smile widened as he placed his hand in the young man's, consummating their new friendship.

"Come," Rabbi Heschel said, as he put his arm around the young man and directed him through the rear door, down a short hallway lined with paintings of the Holy Land. As the two men walked, the rabbi said, "We are Hebrew scholars who study to unlock the door to the secrets of the past. We learn much from archaeology and the ancient writings of our forefathers."

Now, it was Andy's eyes that brightened because he instinctively knew he had come to the right place. The rabbi ushered him into a modest conference room. On a hot plate simmered a pot of tea, of which they each enthusiastically partook. Each man sat directly across a small wooden conference table from the other. As they sipped their tea, the atmosphere grew very casual and friendly. After some polite small talk, Rabbi Heschel asked, "What was it you were saying about some old relics that you found in the Judean wilderness?"

"Yes," Andy answered, "I will show them to you."

He nervously untied his backpack, dug to its bottom, and removed the leather cylinders one by one, laying each on the conference table before the rabbi.

"There they are, all seven," Andy said.

The learned man gazed at the containers then touched each one delicately, much like he would have touched a fragile piece of expensive crystal. The young man quietly observed his every move and expression.

"Hmmm," said the rabbi, "the writing on the leather is definitely ancient Hebrew."

"You can remove the covers from the ends of that one . . . and that one," said Andy, as he pointed toward two separate containers.

"Very interesting," the rabbi said, removing the caps. "This is a matter for our expert staff here, for it may take months, or even years, before the contents of these tubes are removed and translated into English. I think these are old scrolls that are the work of an ancient scribe. Our task will be both methodical and difficult due to their brittle condition. We must proceed with extreme care to maintain their value."

"Value?" asked the young man.

"Archaeological . . . and possibly monetary," the rabbi answered.

"Monetary?" Andy responded without thinking. "I have no money. How much must I pay for your services, as well as the services of your colleagues?"

Rabbi Heschel looked into the wide eyes of the young man with penetrative power, searching to see the soul of an honorable person. His silent concentration was of such intensity that it made his guest feel ill at ease.

"Let us assume that the scrolls do have value," he said in a deliberate manner. "If you will permit us to retain them in our museum for further study, say, for a year or so, then you will pay nothing." He lowered his chin and looked over his reading glasses at his guest.

Andy somberly contemplated his proposition, and then said, "You have my agreement."

"Good," said the rabbi as he piled the leather cylinders together to carry them from the conference room. He then stuck out his right hand toward his guest while rising from his chair. The young man rose, took his host's hand, shook it vigorously, and said, "I plan to leave New York soon and return to Allegheny City, Pennsylvania, where I grew up. I will find employment there and await word from you regarding my scrolls."

Andy bent over the conference table, picked up a pencil, and scribbled on a note pad. "Here," he said, as he handed the paper to the rabbi, "is an address where you can contact me when you finish."

"Most surely," said the learned man as he bowed politely and smiled.

The young man shouldered his backpack and the rabbi accompanied him to the front door. As he left the premises, the whiskered man wished him "Godspeed."

—w—

Andy found a job as a railroad clerk in Allegheny City. Almost seven months passed before a large brown, bulky envelope postmarked New York, New York, arrived at his boarding house. His hands shook as he clumsily tore the envelope open and removed a half-inch thick stack of paper.

The first page was a handwritten message that said:

My dear Andy,

Regretfully, I have both good news and bad news for you. Hopefully you will understand.

Our work of translating the Hebrew scrolls is now complete. The task was not easy, but it was rewarding. Due to the passage of centuries, we found each of the scrolls deteriorated and difficult to unroll because of its brittleness. However, with time and patience, we overcame those obstacles.

It is our opinion that the scrolls are most valuable. The imprinting of the Hebrew text was cast on long thin sheets of gold, making the monetary value of the scrolls extraordinary.

Their contents are extraordinary also. We estimate that they were written sometime between 1000 and 900 B.C., which falls in the Solomonic Period of Hebrew history. Although we cannot be certain, we feel that the text could very well be the work of the great Solomon himself. If so, this alone makes the golden scrolls priceless in archaeological circles.

The single thread of wisdom imparted throughout the text concerns wealth: how to acquire it, accumulate it, multiply it, and enjoy it. It clearly sets forth all the answers that you traveled to the Judean wilderness to find.

Upon completion of the translation, I placed your golden scrolls on display in our museum where they would remain readily available for additional studies that would be necessary to give the find genuine creditability. This was done in accordance with the verbal agreement between the two of us. I am grieved to report that your golden scrolls were stolen from the museum. In the dead of night, thieves broke in without detection and removed a silver chalice, some Roman coins, and the golden scrolls. The authorities have diligently sought to capture the criminals, but to no avail. I shall keep you apprised of any new developments.

I am enclosing copies of the English translation of the golden scrolls that were not taken. I trust that their message shall be of some benefit and consolation to you.

I pray that God will give you the wisdom and understanding of Psalm 37.

With warm regards,
Rabbi Abraham Heschel

Andy sat motionless, momentarily stunned. He had dreamed of acquiring riches from the sale of his scrolls. Now, nothing was left but the worthless paper he held in his hands. He hoped for a fortune lost; discouragement consumed him.

Dusk fell rapidly, casting long shadows through two large windows where Andy sat. The boarding house had few frills. However, his bedroom had the luxury of an overstuffed chair where he sometimes whiled away a lonely evening by reading or dreaming of possibilities.

Being of Scottish descent, he was not one to dwell for long on his misfortune. His grandfather, and father, had instilled in him an old saying, "If life gives you a lemon, use it to make lemonade." He wholeheartedly believed in the principle.

Gradually, his despair waned, but one paragraph of the rabbi's letter continued to haunt him: "The single thread of wisdom imparted throughout the text concerns wealth: how to acquire it, accumulate it, multiply it, and enjoy it. It clearly sets forth all the answers for which you traveled to the Judean wilderness to find."

Andy thought, "Could it be that God used a Bedouin shepherd to bring me the answer to my prayers? Is it possible that the message of the golden scrolls was meant for me?"

Suddenly, the significance of his wilderness experience came to him. During all of those difficult days at the oasis at En-gedi, the answers he had so earnestly sought were in his backpack. He felt somewhat ashamed he had not considered that possibility. Then he remembered what the old Catholic priest had said: "God answers prayer, and He is faithful to those who love Him."

Adrenaline surged through him. A quiet tender voice whispered that in his hands he held the key that unlocks the door to the abundant life. He lay the rabbi's letter aside and began to read.

II

—✦—

*What genuine value
is a golden vase
if it is brimming
with tears?*

—✦—

THE SCROLL
NUMBERED ONE

—⚇—

Money Mentality

The words of the wisest and the richest man in the world, to all who seek the abundant life. I have done everything that my soul desired.

I acquired great wealth; gained universal fame; sought pleasure in wine and sex; built grand works by day and pursued levity by night; planted trees, orchards, gardens, and vineyards; bred prize horses, cattle, sheep, and goats; created reservoirs for watering my fields and animals; had numerous servants and maidens to do my bidding; enjoyed the delights of fine music and the rapturous singing voices of men and women; possessed land reaching farther than my eyes could see; lived in a palace befitting my position; gathered riches piled so high they touched the ceiling of my treasury; undertook noteworthy philanthropic causes; aspired to intellectual heights greater than any other man.

Whatsoever my eyes desired I did not keep from them. Anything my heart wished for I gave to it. I denied myself nothing. Because my work was my life, it was therefore given highest priority. I

23

rejoiced in all of my accomplishments, which were my reward for all my labor.

In time, I found it impossible to satisfy the incessant desires of my soul. I was like the man who has an enormous hole in his heart, and who believes that if he fills it up with enough things, his emptiness will vanish. So, I put more things into the hole than anyone can imagine: more work, exotic pleasures, delicate food, exquisite wine, elegant robes, gold chains, diamond rings, sensual relationships, exciting travel, and witty friends. But nothing I did sealed the hole or eliminated the emptiness there. All was pure vanity. My soul never once ceased to torment me.

Then it occurred to me to seek wisdom. In my search, I found that wisdom is different from intelligence, for wisdom advocates common sense and good judgment based on principle, while intelligence stimulates man's ability to think abstractly and manipulate ideas and events according to human ingenuity. Wisdom is immutable and eternal, while intelligence is transmutable and ephemeral. Mine was a life of intellectual pursuits, void of wisdom. Then I discerned the cause of the hole in my heart.

Once my search ended, I chased after wisdom with every ounce of my being. My appetite for truth knew no boundaries or limits. In my soul, I purposed to become wise. Soon I perceived that respect for the Lord is the beginning of wisdom and that only fools scorn its instruction. The realization came to me that I had been the fool of all fools.

My contemplation of wisdom revealed that man is a trichotomous being composed of body, soul, and spirit. This revelation disclosed that I had lived dichotomously, without benefit of the power of the spirit. I chose to correct this aberration by admitting my imperfection before the Lord and asking the Most High to fill me with Divine Spirit. I exercised my free will, electing to follow the Way. Only then did I experience bona fide freedom, meaning, and purpose. This I definitely know: once I was only part of a man and now I am whole.

The Scroll Numbered One

It is impossible to satisfy the body and soul, unless the spirit is also present. Whereas the body and soul seek self-gratification, the spirit links the finite with the infinite and satisfies man's innate longing for Divine bonding with his Heavenly Father. Wisdom taught me that balance between body, soul, and spirit is essential to attaining a happy and successful life. Thus, I encourage every man who seeks the abundant life to seek wisdom first, for wisdom is of the Lord.

My experience taught me that money alone cannot and will not bring inner peace, happiness, and fulfillment. However, neither can a person find contentment, joy, and meaning while living in the midst of impoverishment. Wisdom dictates that the solution to this dilemma, which is common to man, is to strive to become the kind of person who respects and attracts money. He is the sort of individual whom I call a True Person because he perceives and understands the comprehensiveness of true riches, which entail health, wealth, honesty, purpose, labor, diligence, knowledge, morality, benevolence, faith, love, peace, joy, and spirituality. True riches are superior to materialism by definition, just as a True Person is superior to the selfish greedy man. The True Person ultimately finds the true riches of the abundant life.

If you strive to be a True Person, opportunity and consequently money await you wherever you go, for you will be blessed because of your personal attributes. Who you are does not matter—rather, what you are within is important. Strive to be true to yourself, your spouse, children, mother, father, relatives, friends, associates, leaders, and, above all, your Maker. Your character becomes your seal of approval among men. Thus, it is universal law that the True Person alone shall reap the abundant life.

What do you need to do to be a True Person? Live by the infallible laws of Divine Authority instead of the fallible mandates of society. Acknowledge the existence of God, who has dominion over everything that exists throughout the vast cosmic expanse. Follow the wisdom of the Sacred Writings to guide you in the business of life.

25

Make the most of your earthly sojourn by living a balanced existence. Exercise love and respect for both God and man, as well as the creatures that inhabit the earth and seas, and the growing things that bestow lavish beauty or spring forth with their fruits.

Rise above the base human characteristics of greed and envy, thus making it impossible for you to misuse money entrusted to you. Your conscience dictates that you must use your riches for good instead of evil.

Be aware that a burial shroud has no pockets. Enjoy personal contentment whether your purse is full or empty. Do not permit your financial circumstances to assume such a high degree of importance in your life that you become enslaved by things which rob you of your inner peace and virtuous priorities. Envision money with awe and respect, realizing that it can be the cruelest of masters or the most excellent of slaves.

I established for myself the following creed, which I strive to keep and live as a True Person. This creed reflects a befitting attitude toward money, which you should accept, commit to memory, and consciously apply. Then, day by day and little by little, the creed shall permeate your whole being and become a dynamic force of your nature.

The True Person's Creed

I. I will be fruitful and earn money, to labor six days and rest the seventh, to make money multiply as a grain of corn multiplies when planted in fertile soil, and to gain dominion over the power of money's essence, so that my riches may be used for worthy purposes.

II. I will refrain from the love of money, for such passion causes every sort of iniquity to manifest from the heart, attracting weighty troubles.

III. I will respect and follow the higher laws of Divine order, which bring about the fulfillment of my worthy aspirations by making my efforts fruitful and by giving me increase and dominion regarding monetary matters.

IV. I will walk in the counsel of wise men who possess a special gift for managing money and have the experience of many bountiful harvests.

V. I will not pursue ill-gotten monetary gains, for such profits bear an inescapable curse that is a thousandfold greater than the misery of living in poverty.

VI. I will enact every monetary transaction with honesty and integrity, so that my heart may remain pure and my mind content that I might lie down in peace and sleep in safety.

VII. I will refrain from passion for wine, pleasure, and luxury, for they are not conducive to making my purse fat and my fortune grow.

VIII. I will always measure the value of my fellow man with far greater importance than the temporal value of my riches.

IX. I will respect the authority of the laws of the land, under God, regarding the corporeal matters of life.

X. I will let a humble spirit be my hallmark, rejecting the temptation to become puffed up with pride and brimming with haughtiness because of my affluence.

XI. I will be generous in all ways, choosing not to hoard riches that would be detrimental to me and a grievous evil toward mankind.

XII. I acknowledge that the Almighty owns everything that exists, including all of the wealth of the world and, therefore, assumes the responsibility that ownership invokes; consequently, my primary aim is to be God's spiritual possession, for all of the other details of life shall then be orderly and blessed.

I have made the ultimate goal of my life the challenge of becoming a True Person, and this superior vision has enabled me to attract riches as the honeybee is drawn to the honeysuckle. I have found that by being true to the creed, the creed will be true to me. The same applies for you.

Techniques and methods change, but principles never do. The way things are done and the means of doing them constantly evolve due to our predisposition for innovation, but the universal laws that govern the existence of things are immutable. Therefore, changing techniques and methods should be welcomed if the change is for the betterment of mankind, but tampering with eternal principles invites unwelcome consequences.

Some misguided people, as well as those who blindly follow them, earnestly seek to disprove or circumvent the ageless laws of Higher Authority, especially the law of sowing and reaping. Not once has a man ever sowed good and reaped bad, nor has he ever sowed bad and reaped good. Truth dictates that good reaps good and bad reaps bad. To think otherwise is the equivalent of chasing the wind. However, man never ceases to attempt to do so and, therefore, never ceases to fail, which is all so wearisome and so unnecessary.

Your attitude toward money is important. You must desire money for honorable reasons before it can come to you and bless your life. Worthy ideals, properly pursued, foster healthy self-esteem and attract riches. Unprincipled desires such as greed, envy, and self-gratification may bring riches, but such low-minded purposes also bring many troubles and much heartache. My advice to you is to develop an earnest desire for money in order to aspire to numerous noble deeds.

I beseech you to cautiously cultivate genuine respect for money, for it is laborious to acquire, but effortless to lose. It has the inherent potential for both good and evil. Within its nature lies the potential power to build and to destroy, to succeed and to fail. It is your attitude toward money and what you do with it that determines whether the outcome of your life will be successful.

I encourage you to learn to respect money in the same way that my horsemen respect the fine stallions that fill my stables. These horsemen must have splendid mounts to swiftly take them from place to place, fleeing the frequent dangers of life in the desert or to engage enemies of the kingdom by utilizing the element of surprise. These magnificent animals can run like the wind. However, the selective breeding that makes these horses fleet afoot also produces a fierce combative instinct. Even after their spirit is conquered by my expert horsemen, there remains a remnant of the trait that defies subjugation.

Therefore, my horsemen show uncommon respect for these thoroughbreds because they are necessary to survive and to maintain superiority over desert foes. These animals also have the innate capacity to inflict serious injury upon their keepers. Thus, my horsemen clearly understand the nature of the beasts and give them all the respect they so profoundly deserve.

The nature of these stallions is homologous with the nature of money. Both have the inherent potential to serve their keepers well. But each also has the inherent potential to inflict harm if either is treated carelessly and without due respect. Within both the stallion and money lies the equivocal possibility for both good and evil, the consequence of which is the responsibility of their keeper.

Hear me well: he who would learn proper respect for money should first learn to be a True Person. You will quickly discover that unless you willingly strive to live a life of truth, profound knowledge shall always exceed your grasp and, therefore, you shall never acquire the wisdom necessary to understand the mysterious ways of money.

—⟋⟋⟍—

An oracle to remember:

*The wise respect the value of money and keep close watch
as their purses fatten, but fools who become affluent
squander their money and know not the value of wisdom.*

III

—⟊—

To be truly rich, a person must acknowledge that money is a sacred trust from God to be employed wisely and not wasted.

—⟊—

THE SCROLL
NUMBERED TWO

———〰〰———

Financial Beginnings

A ll financial beginnings are difficult, but the future rewards for displaying persistence while in the midst of difficulties far outweigh the unpleasantness of the sacrifices required. Hear me well: when you begin your quest to acquire riches there are certain *Rules of Financial Beginnings* that you must learn and apply in order to initiate the habitual wealth building skills, philosophical dynamics, and financial momentum necessary to ultimately set you apart from the masses as one of those special people upon whom fortune smiles.

The rules, just three in number, are as follows.

Rule I

The man who would be rich cannot have both money and material things as he begins his quest to earn his fortune.

Becoming wealthy requires making difficult choices regarding the money that fills your purse. The words save and spend are not compatible allies in the battle to triumph over scarcity and impoverishment. If you spend all that you earn simply to acquire things, then you shall enjoy plenteous things but you will never know the security of financial independence. To the contrary, if you keep your temptation to spend well in hand and strive to save, you will in time accumulate much wealth and, ultimately, have both a fat purse that never empties and the things you desire. To put it more simply, if you are obsessed with having material things, you shall never have riches, but if you purpose to accumulate money, you shall one day be able to have the material things that you desire also.

The latter choice is the choice of the wise. All financial beginnings require sacrifice, which must be made either early in life or during the sunset years. Sacrifice made early in life brings a reward of many satisfying days, while the consequence of sacrifice made at the end of life is unending struggle, lack, and want. Make your sacrifice now, so that you may enjoy affluence all of your remaining days on earth.

Rule II

The man who would be rich must form the habit of keeping his rightful share of all that he earns.

If you toil laboriously to continuously fill your purse with money, but discover that you accumulate little because you do not pay yourself a fitting portion of your earnings, you are engaging in folly. Keep for yourself a minimum of one coin from every ten you earn. This is a fundamental principle that you must follow if you are ever to achieve financial independence. Once you pay yourself, then divide what remains to pay tribute to your government and meet all of your other financial obligations. Your financial difficulties shall be overcome only if you practice paying yourself first, and then paying the amount left over to others. There can be no compromise regarding this fundamental principle.

You may say, "But if there is not now enough money to pay the merchants or to provide necessities for my loved ones, how can I possibly pay myself first? This would make the merchants and money lenders indeed disgruntled." I say, let them be disgruntled if they choose to be. Your only obligation is to pay them regularly their fair portion of the available funds on hand after you pay yourself. Do not be surprised if they object and threaten you with all manner of retribution when you cannot pay each of them as much as they prefer. After all is said and done, they will gladly accept punctual payments that are established on your own terms. Be fair with your terms and as good fortune begins to smile on you and, in turn, you begin to earn more, pay them more. Once each of them is paid in full, never again permit yourself to become a participant in such folly. My counsel to you is this: learn to live free of all debt.

Rule III

The man who would be rich must seek wise counsel and exercise good judgment that will make his savings beget limitless amounts of its own kind in the future.

Capital has a prolific propagating nature. Money can beget money, and its offspring can beget more. There is no end to its potential to procreate. One acorn planted in fertile soil and properly nurtured becomes a thousand forests. So it is with money.

Our mandate from God is to be fruitful, multiply, and have dominion. This great mandate encompasses the whole of life, including the financial realm. Some men earn a fortune during their lifetime and therefore honor the mandate of the Almighty to be fruitful. But most fail to honor His mandate to multiply that which they earn and therefore never attain dominion over their own financial affairs. This being the unfortunate situation, I implore you to resolve to be different than all those who fail so miserably. I encourage you to steadfastly embrace each separate dimension of this supreme decree which exhorts you to be fruitful, to multiply, and to take dominion with specific regard to your monetary matters, if you genuinely desire to find a permanent cure for your lean purse. This Divine mandate is the only cure in existence that lasts a lifetime.

Hear me well: you must learn quickly that a man becomes fruitful by expending singularly directed mental energy and the sweat of his brow into his lifework. If you are fortunate enough that yours is a labor of love, so much the better. Uniting both mental and physical effort into singleness of purpose creates an omnipotent force of fulfillment.

The amount of wisely conceived mental and physical effort that you put into your work determines your productiveness and, consequently, the quantity of your earnings. Six days of arduous labor, with the seventh set aside for mental, physical, and spiritual renewal, should become common practice in the beginning. Self-discipline is essential to the development of good work habits. Remember this: in the beginning you make your habits, but in the end your habits make you. Form the habit of planning your work. Discipline yourself to work according to your plan. Never fail to include in your plan time to devote to your family's pleasure and counsel, for your family is like a priceless jewel.

Avoid the temptation to lend your money to the enticing allure of get-rich-quick schemes. Realize that chasing instantaneous riches is a sure way to end up with an empty purse. Flee from the bewitchment of speculative ventures that promise unprecedented gains in exchange for the use of your hard earned savings, for the risk of loss is too great. Conversely, forgo the endless number of opportunities to lend your savings to those who would fail to pay you justly for its use. Seek and find a place of safe keeping for your money that will reward you fairly and ensure that your savings grow consistently.

The Scroll Numbered Two

As you set out to build your fortune, seek the advice of one having hair of white, who successfully counsels the wealthy of your city. A counselor who has successful experience knows where to employ your hard earned savings, so that it shall be on the pathway of growth and return to you much more of its own kind. A wise counselor will make your profits increase while you sleep in peace. But never, under any circumstances, trust your advisor to the degree that you leave the management of your money solely in his hands, without the benefit of your own recommendations. Keep constant vigilance over your fortune as it multiplies, regardless of the impressive qualifications of your chosen advisor.

I once knew a rich man named Hafid, who lived in an imposing mansion in Damascus. He was a successful seller of goods who labored long and saved much, then unwisely entrusted the multiplication of his fortune to an unqualified counselor who foolishly squandered it in very risky ventures. Due to the counselor's imprudent decisions, Hafid lost everything he owned. My heart went out to him for he was forced to start anew. He never again regained the affluence that he once had known.

Unfortunately, the story of Hafid is commonplace, for it is repeated generation after generation. Will man ever become wise to the pitfall of such folly? This I doubt. However, there is a profound lesson in such an experience because money has never been spent to so great an advantage than when it is foolishly lost, for through such an experience a man purchases prudence. Money is time-laden and toilsome to acquire, but sometimes becomes mercurial in the hands of well meaning advisors and therefore can swiftly take flight like a frightened grouse.

In order to attain dominion over your financial affairs, you must first achieve financial freedom, which simply means liberation from personal need and want caused by the scarcity of money to provide your ongoing financial necessities. It means acquiring relief from worry regarding the essentials of life for your loved ones, plus having some of life's little comforts as well. Financial freedom is achieved through the habitual application of the *Rules of Financial Beginnings*. Dominion occurs when enduring financial freedom is attained.

Hafid successfully built wealth, but he failed to maintain it because he never assumed dominion over his monetary affairs. Dominion means exercising supreme authority over every material blessing with the guidance of wisdom. The source of authentic wisdom is the Sacred Scriptures that were given for our enlightenment by our Creator. These inspired writings reveal everything we need to know concerning the art of skillful living and financial success.

I counsel you to follow the *Rules of Financial Beginnings* and be fruitful, multiply, and take dominion over your material blessings. Begin immediately, regardless of your present circumstances. Do not procrastinate, for tomorrow never comes. Tomorrow is the fictitious retreat where failures live. Be wise, live one day at a time, do your very best each day, and eventually your treasury will overflow and your dwelling shall abound with happiness.

—⟋⟍—

An oracle to remember:

You must save a meaningful portion of all that you earn and employ it to work for you and to provide a never ending stream of income.

IV

—❧—

A man without a budgetary plan becomes fair game for every predator in the financial jungle.

—❧—

THE SCROLL
NUMBERED THREE

—ᵚ—

Budget Management

Two score and two years ago a young man from Babylon came to me for counsel. His name was Arkad and he was bright and ambitious, but he had a serious failing: he could not manage the coins properly that regularly filled his purse. He confided to me, "There is hardly enough money in my purse to pay everyone to whom payment is due, and there is never any surplus to provide for my golden years." He found his situation most disheartening and asked me for a solution.

I assured Arkad that, although his problem appeared grave to him, there was a simple yet demanding answer. I told him that I had counseled many who suffered from the same dilemma. The five lessons that follow were my counsel to him and all others who had come to me before that day, as well as my counsel to you.

Lesson One

The money that regularly fills your purse is elusive to possess, for it tends to flow through your fingers like the waters of the Salt Sea, leaving only residue that makes your hands in need of pure cleansing. Without such cleansing, your hands remain unfit to partake of the bread on your table. So it is with your bad habits concerning management of money. Unless your bad habits are cleansed, you shall never be fit to partake of the banquet table of life.

Hence, you are in dire need of a Budgetary Plan to govern over your financial affairs. Attempting to sail the sea of life without a plan is folly and much like a ship at sea without a rudder. The purpose of a Budgetary Plan is to keep account of all revenue in relation to all expenditures, allowing for efficient money management and promoting thrift. If you are wise, you will make use of a budget as routinely as you practice eating, drinking, and sleeping. A budget sets you free from pecuniary bondage and gives you authority over your financial destiny. Living without a Budgetary Plan invites financial problems. Such a grave mistake can lead to financial failure.

Every man must bear the burden of having more desires than he can possibly gratify. The appetite of the soul is indeed insatiable. A person who yields to unrestricted personal desires becomes a prisoner of the world's system that enslaves the masses in a dungeon of debt. Therefore, you must not allow yourself to be deceived and enticed to take part in such unmitigated indiscretion. You must learn to control your desires if the effect of a Budgetary Plan is to be financial freedom. As you begin your mission to conquer your bad money-management habits, you must keep your desires simple and definite, and consistent with the objectives of your Budgetary Plan. You will accomplish your purpose step by step.

You must also learn contentment during each station of your life, for this is wisdom. Contentment is a product of the heart to be relished whether your financial fortune flourishes or takes a turn for the worse. But there is one thing for certain: your financial fortune will not remain the same throughout your life, so prepare yourself for inevitable ups and downs. If you resolve to live by sound principles, your financial matters will not destroy your contentment, for contentment is a conscious choice. Be content if you have much, or if you have little. Contentment is a blessing in and of itself.

The world will continuously create distractions, obstacles, and problems that can destroy contentment. There is no end to the appealing temptations that make desire burn in your bosom, so be on guard, for a discontented heart is open to every sort of folly. Choose contentment, reject the enticements of the world, and live your life in peace and harmony.

How much of your earnings did you save last month? Last year? If your situation is like that of the masses, you saved little, or nothing. If this is so, you are a fool. The world's system holds you captive to your irrational desires and you provide handsomely for everyone's financial security but your own. If this is true, then you must rectify your situation.

A well conceived Budgetary Plan, aggressively initiated and followed through, is the solution to your predicament. Remember, the purpose of such a plan is to fatten your purse perpetually and bless you with financial freedom. Such a plan enables you to provide well for necessities and have enough money left over to gratify some of your desires.

To attain financial freedom you must neither ignore nor flee from your financial problems. To the contrary, you must face them boldly and solve them. To do so requires courage and determination. Why? Because order is a Divine decree of the universe. Order directs the celestial bodies throughout the vastness of the heavens, guides the complex cycles of animal and plant life, and even governs something as insignificant in the universal scheme of things as the activities of man. The potential for order exists, but you must choose to let it govern your life and financial affairs.

A Budgetary Plan must be flexible and applicable to today, as well as tomorrow. The order created through the implementation of a Budgetary Plan brings freedom of the heart. Where there is financial order, financial success will follow hidden amidst the bountiful blessings bestowed by the Almighty.

Lesson Two

The man who cannot live on ten gold pieces per month would find it impossible to live on one hundred gold pieces per month. Such a man must face reality. His problem does not lie in the amount of money he earns but, instead, in his inability to live within his means. If you habitually spend more than you earn, you sow the ill wind of financial misfortune and will reap a whirlwind of financial trouble and disgrace. You will become rich in proportion to the number of material excesses that you can eliminate from your life.

Do not confuse necessary living expenses with compulsive desires for materialistic pleasures. If you fail to learn this principle, what you define as necessary living expenses will grow boundlessly as your income continues to increase due to your productivity. Choose to maintain the same standard of living until financial freedom smiles on you.

Spending money before you have it is not prudent. A gold piece in your hand has more power than two that have not yet come to you. Bargain from a position of strength with money in hand instead of a position of weakness using money you do not yet possess. Money in the hand of a wise man has much might. Thoughtfully consider your established habits regarding how you manage your money, for therein lie the secrets of eliminating material excesses and seizing control of your financial destiny.

Lesson Three

If you desire to be rich, you must learn and practice the following precepts to guide you to a happy and productive life:

- A charitable heart is essential to finding true riches.
- The wise man uses money as a tool to symbolically cultivate his soil and plant seeds, so that his harvest shall be plentiful.
- Money is not the end in and of itself, but it represents the means to a worthy end if it is employed wisely.

44

- Good fortune seeks out the man who saves a minimum of one-tenth of all that he earns and wisely employs his savings to produce more of its own kind.

- Financial security blesses the man who creates an unending stream of income adequate to provide for his future budgetary requirements.

- A man must pay each of his debts in full, while exercising complete punctuality in the process.

- The responsible man wisely engages one well versed in the laws of the land to write for him a plan that will ensure the proper distribution of his estate upon his death and in accordance with his wishes.

- The prudent man respects the worth of money and will not squander it to purchase excessive luxuries that rapidly depreciate in value.

- A wise man learns to despise debt because it is an evil that has the potential to destroy his life.

- The man in quest of his fortune should build a stable, sufficient source of income before he invests in building the dwelling of his dreams.

- Both thought and labor are necessary ingredients to ensuring financial success; slothfulness brings poverty.

- A wise man positions himself in the pathway of opportunity and in the midst of progress so his fortune shall have the best chance to grow.

Lesson Four

The man who does not have definite financial goals and a plan for their accomplishment has no more chance of becoming financially independent than a camel has of learning to fly. Financial goals are but financial dreams on which the dreamer places specific deadlines.

If you desire to become rich, you must commit your goals to writing in the form of a Budgetary Plan that is identifiable, measurable, and attainable. Budget your finances so the money that regularly fills your purse is sufficient to pay for the necessities of life, eliminate debt, remit taxes to the government, share with others who are in need, and provide some worthwhile pleasures to satisfy your desire for enjoyment without spending more than nine-tenths of all that you earn.

Many men know how to earn money, but not one in a thousand knows how to spend it wisely. To develop a successful Budgetary Plan and attain financial freedom, you must resolve to do the following by faith and without questioning why:

I. Analyze your present financial situation and make a written record of every expenditure. This will reveal to what purposes your hard earned money is applied.

II. Pledge to live your life and manage your financial affairs supported only by the cash you have on hand.

III. Conquer the adversaries of sound money management: First, the false conception that more is better; second, the temptation to use easy credit to delay the unpleasantness of making difficult financial decisions that must be made in order to set financial affairs on the proper course; third, the failure to keep one-tenth of all income to employ and create more of its own kind; and fourth, the mistake of increasing spending when income increases.

IV. Make the creation of surplus your supreme goal. There is greater pleasure and fulfillment in the creation of surplus than there is in spending it.

V. Provide for both short-range and long-range goals in your Budgetary Plan. Short-range goals should be established for each day, week, and month. Long-range goals should be made to put you on course to achieve your dreams beyond one year. Your

Budgetary Plan must remain flexible, so that it may be revised to your best advantage as you gain valuable experience with the passage of time.

VI. Continually study to make yourself wiser and more skilled in the effective ways of money management.

VII. Be determined to follow a Budgetary Plan that allocates payments from all the income you earn in the succeeding order and the ensuing manner:

- *First,* give a generous portion of your income to worthy causes and to those less fortunate who are in genuine need, for your good-hearted generosity will become the source of your greatest blessings.

- *Second,* pay yourself a minimum of one-tenth of all that you earn, and safely employ the payment so that it earns more of its own kind.

- *Third,* pay your rightful share of taxes to your government, so that there will be money enough to support governing the land.

- *Fourth,* provide for the necessities of your family, so that you may respect yourself and have the respect of your spouse and children.

- *Fifth,* pay regularly to reduce your debt until it remains no more.

- *Sixth,* use any money that is left over to satisfy your desire to partake of the pleasures of life for both yourself and your family.

The specific amounts that you allocate for payments should be determined as follows:

- Calculate the amount of *spendable income* available by deducting any taxes, and one-tenth, which you give to help others, then allocate it as follows:

—Keep one-tenth for your savings
—Provide seven-tenths to care for your household
—Pay two-tenths to reduce your debt until it is eliminated

You might think this cannot be done, but it can if you believe that it can. Becoming financially independent sometimes requires sacrifice by doing whatever is expedient in order to accomplish the objective. You can endure any adversity for a short time if the reward for your sacrifice is great enough.

Once financial freedom is achieved, you should reallocate the amount of your spendable income thusly:

- Consider increasing the amount that you share for benevolent purposes according to your increasing abundance
- Provide seven-tenths to care for your household
- Employ the remainder to work for you and return more of its own kind

Never permit your household expenses to exceed seven-tenths of your income. These expenses should include allocations for such items as food, clothing, shelter, household expenses, medicine, entertainment, and recreation. As your income increases in time, you should resolve to live on less than seven-tenths if possible. Thus, keep your standard of living within reasonable limits and utilize the difference, in part, to share with others in need and to employ to bring you more of its own kind. Teach your children these same precepts, so that when they go out into the world they shall be properly prepared to acquire their fair share of all the riches the world has to offer.

When each child grows into adulthood and leaves home or when your dwelling and other possessions are paid for, employ the extra money gained to help others and to multiply itself. Hence, your blessings will grow. Continuously strive to make additional surplus and to make that surplus your slave, which will work for you faithfully so that it begets a stream of future income to keep you financially independent throughout your life and, later, to work for those you love when your earthly walk ends.

—m—

An oracle to remember:

Financial success requires a man to have a plan for spending, as well as for saving, enabling him to create a surplus that he must wisely employ to bring financial freedom for the future.

V

—⚬—

Gold finds its way into the
purse of a man who gives
more and better service,
as surely as the sun
rises in the east.

—⚬—

THE SCROLL
NUMBERED FOUR

—꿈—

Increasing Income

There is a way to consistently increase your income throughout your lifetime. Wise men have followed this way for millenniums. Those who follow it do not stump their toes and fall, for the way is smooth and free from perilous potholes. The way that I speak of is known as the *Principles of the Harvest*, which reveal the basic truths that bring financial growth.

Luck is not a reliable factor in life. It should not be given any serious consideration regarding the process of building wealth. Fortune favors the diligent, who know and apply the *Principles of the Harvest*. Remain true to these precepts and you shall prosper.

The *Principles of the Harvest* are founded upon the universal law of sowing and reaping that governs all that you will or will not be in this life. This law is the predominant governing law of life, here and now, as well as in the future. There is no escape from its power, for it was established by Divine decree. It is profoundly true that *whatsoever a man soweth, that shall he also reap.* This great law applies not only to the whole of life but also to the ambiguous nature of money. If you would be rich, you must live by this great law, giving it the uttermost reverence and respect.

Learn now the *Principles of the Harvest* and let them be your guide to finding your financial destiny.

Principle I

You can do nothing about the yields of past harvests, but you can affect the yields of future harvests.

Every new beginning is difficult because of imperfect financial seeds sowed in the past that shall grow and ripen unto a poor harvest. Nothing can be done about such seeds that are already planted, for they are destined by the law of nature to produce a harvest. In financial matters, if you plant imperfect seeds then you will bear the consequences, for you cannot change what you have already done. However, you can immediately begin planting good financial seeds instead of bad ones and thus change the yield of future harvests from sparsity to abundance. Financial mistakes of the past are events of history that cannot be relived or redone. Yes, we can learn from them, but we cannot change them. The past must be left to sort out its own outcome and ultimate concern must be directed to the present, for the things that are being done currently are the seeds of future harvests.

Principle II

You reap only the same kind of seed that you sow.

Everything that exists springs forth in like manner from that which has existed before. The financial harvest a man reaps is the result of what he purposefully plants. If a man sows wheat, he will reap wheat; if he sows poison, he shall reap poison. The law decreeing that like produces like was handed down from the beginning by the One who created everything that exists. Hear me well: by law, things produce their own kind. And remember: thoughts are also things.

Is it possible that ill-conceived thoughts have led you to develop poor money management habits that are but seeds of financial failure sown in blindness? Is a financial setback that you are currently working through the harvest of bad financial seeds sown sometime in the past? If this is so, you have proven through experience the absolute validity of the law that each thing must produce its own kind. There is no exception to the veracity of this precept. If this were not true, the mere whims of man would make a mockery of the laws of the universe.

If you sow inferior financial seeds, you shall most surely reap an inferior harvest. To the contrary, if you sow quality financial seeds, you shall most definitely reap a quality harvest. Never permit your savings to be exposed to any means of multiplying your wealth that is not founded upon the premise of genuine quality. When your finances are involved, accept nothing inferior; accept nothing mediocre; accept only what is of proven quality. Quality begets its own kind in full unending measure. Let quality be the unwritten code for all your financial affairs.

My counsel is that you should not be deceived by those in financial circles who advocate the mistaken belief that in every instance more is better. Quantity, not quality, is their guiding rule. The truth of the matter is that the importance of quality is paramount. Emphasis on quantity should be of secondary consideration when compared to the advantages of quality. Quality brings the best that life can offer.

Principle III

You plant seeds in one season to be harvested in another season.

In the great universal scheme of things, everything is subject to the order that the Supreme Architect has established. Everything progresses and happens according to its own appointed time and in its own appointed season. Understanding and patience are important attributes you must acquire, or this third principle shall continually be a source of anxiety, frustration and, sometimes, depression.

It is not nature's way for the harvest to spring forth at the instant that seeds are planted, for it takes time for seeds to root, grow, multiply, and mature. Adequate time for growth and propagation is required in between the time for sowing and the time for reaping. What you do with the time in between affects the yield of the harvest. This precious time must be utilized to nurture the growing crop through floods and droughts, harmful diseases, and attacks from destructive insects. You must not succumb to fatigue and weariness during this time. You must persevere. The season of the harvest is the time for reaping. Once the harvest is gathered and the silo is filled to overflowing, there is a reason for much rejoicing and celebration. As it is with seeds planted in a fertile field, so it is also with the challenge of building wealth.

My counsel is that you should not expect miraculous results overnight as you begin your journey toward financial independence. Under the best circumstances, it usually takes from three to five years to accomplish such a commendable pursuit. Do not let the amount of time required bring you discouragement, for much time is needed to allow you to find your special place in the path of opportunity; learn new precepts, form new habits, and develop a new modus operandi. Time allocated to the preceding things is time well invested. Time is indeed precious, so use it wisely.

Principle IV

You will reap a greater harvest than you sow.

The writings of old reveal this secret: "If thou sowest the wind, thou shalt reap a whirlwind." This is a most sobering and important truth, for it is a principle that cuts just like a double-edged sword. This precept applies to sowing success or failure, happiness or unhappiness, and riches or poverty. Nature does not reproduce the same number of seeds that are planted, but instead multiplies them and reproduces them a hundredfold or thousandfold.

For example, a farmer went out to his field to sow and placed one tiny grain of corn in each of the numerous little holes that he dug in the fertile soil. In a few days, many small green sprouts appeared. Next, the sprouts grew into sizable stalks. Then many small shoots began to grow from the stalks, which developed into wee growths having many minuscule new grains of corn, which then matured into full grown ears. As they grew, there appeared another ear, and another, until all the stalks stood tall and were laden with numerous ears replete with golden grain. At harvest time, the farmer surveyed his crop and was bewildered as he remembered how each had begun from a single minute seed. He had sowed sufficiently, but he reaped abundantly. Thus, the veracity of the fourth principle was vividly proven to him. He learned quickly that seeds planted in fertile soil and nourished do not simply produce the same amount of their own kind, but actually produce an abundance of their own kind.

The inherent dynamics of the fourth principle are universal in nature. They are just as applicable to financial matters as they are to the crops of the field. Therein lies a truth that can take you to extraordinary heights of success and fortune or, when improperly applied, can take you into the vast depths of failure and depravation. The choice is yours. Therefore, you must take great care to sow financial seeds that are good, so your bountiful harvest will also be good.

Principle V

The more seeds you sow, the greater the harvest.

A wise farmer who would reap a large harvest must sow many seeds across the length and breadth of many acres. Nature's law dictates that he must sow abundantly if he is to reap exceedingly abundantly.

However, the farmer should wisely exercise caution not to sow more than he can reasonably manage.

My counsel is that if you honestly desire to make a big financial harvest, you must first sow many financial seeds. The money you earn constitutes your seeds, so sow them wisely in many fertile places and they shall return to you much more of their own kind. You must think big and act big if you sincerely want to reap a big harvest. Make a consistent effort to increase your income. Use your increase to continually plant more financial seeds in more acres, that you may always reap greater and greater harvests.

Principle VI

A poor harvest manifests itself on its own, but an abundant harvest only comes to those who persevere.

A young farmer planted his first field of wheat and soon learned that weeds grow profusely on their own while wheat requires much nurturing. He found that growing an abundant harvest is indeed a laborious and time-consuming undertaking. He discovered that if he left his field unattended, weeds flourished and kept sunlight and moisture from the delicate plants, thus inhibiting their growth. Much to his dismay, he also discovered it was necessary to wage constant battle against disastrous blight, ravaging animals, and destructive insects. However, he found his greatest challenge to be the frequent droughts that forced him to transport water from a nearby river just to keep his wheat alive.

The young farmer learned through experience that if he was to celebrate at harvest time, he must persevere relentlessly in order to overcome all the obstacles that stood in his way. He also learned the precept that nothing worthwhile in life is easy. He found that there were many dangerous enemies and destructive elements that he must struggle against and overcome. As time passed, he grew older and wiser and successfully produced many abundant harvests. He came to the conclusion that the many rewards he had received for his perseverance were worth the commitment and effort he had expended.

Hear me well: the moral of the story about the young farmer applies to life in general, as well as to the financial affairs of all men. For you see, the bad in the world is ever present and perpetuates itself, while good is something that must be cultivated, nurtured, and cared for with undying attention. The underlying meaning of this parable relates well to any of life's challenges, such as building a fortune, running a business, raising a family, maintaining important relationships, developing spirituality, and keeping well and physically fit. When anything bad is sown, it comes to harvest on its own. However, when something good is sown, it requires constant attention in order to reap an abundant harvest.

You can transform your problems into building blocks of character if you persevere. How you react to your problems shall determine your success or failure. Generally, great character is something that must be chiseled and shaped from the granite quarries of misfortune. Great character is the reward for persevering in times of adversity and virtue is the offspring of great character. You will never achieve *true* success unless you first possesses character and virtue, for they are the hallmarks of greatness. Your primary objective should be building your character, for character is the only thing you can take with you into eternity.

Alas! You now know the mystery of the *Principles of the Harvest;* be kind to them and they shall be kind to you.

The Miracle of Service

I will teach you the secret of secrets regarding how you can continuously increase your income to grand proportions. You will discover that you were not taught these secrets in your schools of learning, for the world of academe abandoned the teaching of profound knowledge long ago. Once the secrets become yours, share them with others and you shall be blessed.

Here is the key that will open the door to unlimited income for you: *First, you must provide service. Then, you will become successful and the financial rewards will follow.* The secret of secrets is as amazing and yet as simple as the preceding statement.

It does not matter whether you labor in the employment of another or toil solely on behalf of yourself; *service* is the tool you must use to increase your income throughout your life. You will receive financial rewards in direct proportion to the quality and quantity of service that you render to others. Therefore, let your motto become: *Serve and succeed.*

If you earnestly desire to acquire riches and all of the power and influence that riches bring, you must first become a servant. The place to begin your life of service is right where you are at at this moment. Do not procrastinate; start serving now.

To begin, you must free yourself of thoughts of pettiness, prejudice, envy, and selfishness, which are nothing but destructive emotional indulgences that stand in the way of your success. Such thoughts are detrimental to you alone. A person who harbors such thoughts cannot develop a servant's heart. The guiding precept of a servant's heart must be to freely give the unconditional quality and quantity of service to others that you desire to be given unto you. Believing in and following this precept sets you apart from the multitudes who go about their daily tasks stagnated by unprincipled practices, conformity, and mediocrity. Rendering more and better service sets the *Principles of the Harvest* in operation. More and better service plants many seeds of excellent quality across many fields, most of which will take root, grow, multiply, and bring forth an abundant harvest in the proper season.

People will respond to you according to your thoughts and actions toward them. A genuine spirit of service is an unseen force that becomes irresistible to those to whom service is freely and unconditionally given. Even the most calloused people become susceptible to you when service is the instrument used to cut through the layers of their hardened demeanor.

Consistent, good service causes the *Rule of Reciprocity* to take effect. When you do something of value for another person, that person is then compelled to do something of value in return. If you serve others well, you will eventually rise to a station of prominence because all those you have serviced will one day reciprocate in a positive manner.

I vividly recall how Elymus, a seller of goods from Jericho, applied the *Rule of Reciprocity* to his advantage. Elymus earnestly desired that Jonan, the owner of a successful emporium, become his customer. Through the assistance of Ali, a mutual friend, a meeting was arranged. Elymus prepared well. When the two men met, Elymus talked of mutual acquaintances and interests. He then told of his burning desire to render more and better service than any other vendor. He spoke of quality, honesty, hard work, and dedication to his customers. He tantalized Jonan with thoughts of increased profits. He displayed one of his best wool robes made without a seam, with color so rich it would never fade. He showed lambskin sandals with leather so soft they soothed the feet. He exhibited fine linen for turbans, unique silk underthings, and sheer veils imported from Persia.

Jonan graciously complimented Elymus, but he was not interested in any of the vendor's wares, since it was customary for him to purchase all of his goods from his good friend, Imri. Elymus said, "I commend you for your loyalty to a friend. Take the robe and sandals and wear them. They are my gift to you for the extraordinary hospitality you have shown me." Bowing gracefully, he said, "May your life be long and your fortune great," and he withdrew from the presence of Jonan.

Thereafter, every time the seasons changed, Elymus visited with Jonan to cultivate his friendship and provide him with valuable information, always leaving with him a long list that described available merchandise. On special occasions, Elymus sent Jonan pleasant tidings by messengers. He invited him to attend noteworthy festivities as his guest. For his friendship, Elymus asked nothing in return.

Early one spring morning, Jonan went to Elymus, visibly disturbed. He said, "My friend, I have a crisis. Imri has failed to deliver the merchandise I ordered for the summer season. Without it, my emporium shall lose customers and I shall suffer great financial loss." This was the opportunity that Elymus' patience and service had brought. He said, "Jonan, my friend, you have my compassion. The time is short, but I shall do my best to be of assistance in your time of need."

Elymus immediately sent messengers to garment and sandal makers throughout the land. Before the next full moon, the seller of goods had filled Jonan's emporium with quality merchandise purchased at competitive prices. Jonan was elated and grateful. That summer's market was exceedingly profitable.

The moral of this story is that Elymus acquired Jonan as a customer because he had a servant's heart. There are certain attributes that one must develop in order to serve others well:

I.   Loyalty and trustworthiness
II. Strong character tempered by a humble spirit
III. An insatiable desire to listen and learn
IV. A passion to serve others without promise of reward
V.   The discernment to discover needs and meet them
VI. The vision to imagine needs and create them
VII. An extraordinary capacity for work on the behalf of those who are served

Elymus did not become a successful vendor until he first developed a servant's heart. It was not until he gained the aforesaid attributes that his success and, consequently, his fortune began to soar. Therefore, you must understand the paramount importance of service if you are to begin with nothing but desire. Then go forth and build your fortune in the business arena of the world.

Be assured that if you begin providing more and better service, but find that financial rewards from your present vocation do not grow in proportion to the quantity and quality of service you are rendering, you shall then receive financial rewards from unexpected sources that will pay you justly for what you do. Simply demonstrate your faith in the *Principles of the Harvest* by giving more and better service and worrying about nothing; one way or another you will be justly paid what you are worth. Have faith and be diligent; in the proper season your just reward will come. Hear me well: do a good job at what you are doing and the future will take care of itself.

Once you begin your plan to render more and better service, your success will be immediate and lasting, for you will be doing the things that are necessary to make your financial dreams come true. Your peers, and others, will begin to show respect for your success long before your financial harvest comes to fruition. They will discern by your attitude and actions that you are a person destined for lofty heights of accomplishment and prosperity. This is good, for it is important to the yield of your harvest that others perceive you as successful. Success begets success!

Others naturally desire to associate and work with a successful person. You will fulfill their desire, not because of the price of the clothes you wear or the size of the dwelling in which you live, but because of the quality and quantity of service you render. The unique message they will receive from your servant's heart is, "I am here to render you more and better service than you can get from anyone else."

When riches come, they come in such abundance that you will wonder where they were hiding during all those years your purse was lean. Now you know the secret of secrets that shall guide you to financial independence: *Service, Success,* then *Money,* in that order.

—w—

An oracle to remember:

The mission of a man who desires to perpetually increase his income must center on providing more and better service to his fellowman, which will ultimately reward him with many abundant financial harvests.

VI

—⁘—

The man destined to be rich
must protect the potential
value of his future
earning power.

—⁘—

THE SCROLL
NUMBERED FIVE

—m—

Protecting Wealth

I once knew an alchemist named Demas who had an obsession for finding a way to turn base metals into pure gold. He was a jolly robust man who fancied his long black beard and always wore a sheepskin apron. He spent many intense hours in his laboratory.

One day, Demas was busy mixing a formula into a solution. He moved liquids and powders here and there on his worktable, mixing some of them together as his formula required. He accidentally knocked over one of the vials of solution, spilling it into the fire he kept burning in a small kiln. When the solution splashed upon the hot coals it made a loud hissing sound and then exploded into dancing reddish-yellow flames, filling the room with a cloud of dusty gray smoke.

Demas suffered minor burns on his hands and arms. Injured and frightened, he fled through the door out into the fresh air where he stood gasping for his next breath. He was thankful he had not been killed, for the explosion was of such magnitude it seriously damaged his laboratory.

Smoke billowed out the door and windows. Once it cleared enough to allow Demas to survey the damage, he cautiously made his way back inside. Fortunately, the damage was not irreparable. Yet he was still fretful because he realized that it would take several days to tidy up the disarray. So, the following morning he unwillingly began the unpleasant task that lay before him.

Being a happy man, Demas whistled as he worked—the faster he whistled, the faster he worked. He took time away from his task only to eat and sleep. Three and one-half days sped past. The last thing he tended to was cleaning the kiln, which was covered with black soot that emitted a most peculiar odor. As he meticulously scrubbed each stone of the kiln, he saw an unusual tiny bubble-like object fixed on top of one of the snuffed coals. The appearance of the tiny object made him very curious, so he picked that specific coal out of the kiln and gently placed it on the hearth.

Demas continued cleaning his laboratory. Once he was done, he was weary but not too weary to attempt to satisfy his curiosity about the tiny object attached to the coal on the kiln hearth. He stood across the room looking at it. It was so small he could hardly see it from that distance.

Consequently, Demas walked over and picked it up and placed it on the worktable. He delicately removed the object from the coal. It was no larger than a mustard seed. Its color was a motley mixture of black, orange, and yellow. He noticed that, although it had cooled from being in the fire, it mysteriously created a warm sensation at the spot where it lay in his palm. He had never experienced anything like this. He took the tiny object and put it in a small wooden box for safe keeping.

Upon entering his laboratory the next day, Demas picked up the wooden box and took it in front of a large window in order to have the advantage of the morning light. The interior of the box was charred black just as if it had been exposed to a smoldering fire overnight. In the midst of the charred receptacle was the tiny motley colored object. He asked himself, "Could this harmless looking speck of something possibly have done this?"

Suddenly, Demas received a flash of inspiration. He sat down and sketched the plans of a strange looking contraption to be carved from granite, which had channels running through its center from top to bottom and side to side. It was two cubits square and had a chamber in the middle in which the tiny object was to be permanently placed. He designed a way for water to circulate through the channel that ran from side to side.

Next, Demas developed a plan that detailed the process of refining iron from ore, then routing the molten iron through the channel that went from top to bottom. Intuition revealed to him that when the molten iron flowed past the tiny object in the chamber its molecular nature would be changed from that of iron to gold. As the liquefied gold flowed on through the channel filled with circulating water, it would cool, harden, and pass from the opening in the bottom in the form of shiny nuggets. The alchemist did not understand every detail about his plan, but something told him that he had designed a device of monumental significance.

Knowing he had the plan for inventing a machine with great potential value, he worked tirelessly to bring his dream to fruition. Hours, then days passed before his dream was realized. When he finished, he stepped back and beheld his masterful work.

He named his contraption the *Money Machine* and he named the mysterious tiny object Terrennium, which was uniquely rare because he was never able to recreate the same molecular reaction again. Therefore, that small amount—no larger than the head of a pin—was all the Terrennium that ever existed.

The alchemist then initiated the process to turn iron into gold. The Money Machine hissed, sputtered, and fumed. In a matter of moments, a bright gold nugget fell into the basket he had placed to catch it. Then another and another. Quickly, Demas stopped the Money Machine.

He said to himself, "There are those who would attempt to steal the Money Machine if they learned of it. Therefore, I must protect it at all costs, for it is worth much. I will go to my wise friend who knows much about financial matters, tell him of my discovery, and seek his counsel."

So Demas brought his problem to me, his lifelong friend. He knew that I have extensive experience in financial matters and also wealth enough to prove the worth of my wisdom.

The alchemist told me of his discovery and explained his fear of economic loss if something unexpected happened to the Money Machine. I told Demas, "Let us go to your laboratory, so that I may see this miracle that you say can make gold from iron."

We proceeded immediately to Demas' laboratory, where he demonstrated all that he had told me. Upon seeing a pure gold nugget the size of a child's fist fall into the basket, I shouted, "Amazing! Simply amazing! Demas, my old friend, you have unlocked the mystery of alchemy. Amazing!" My excitement was evident.

"I am rich!" Demas yelled with exuberance.

I picked up the large nugget and wallowed it around in the palm of my hand as I inspected it carefully. "The gold is perfect," I said. "Demas, you have made the discovery of all discoveries. Surely you must find a way to protect yourself against the potential loss of the future income that the Money Machine will produce for you."

I said, "Demas, my old friend, I think that I have discerned a way to protect the Money Machine against loss. As you know, I am an exceedingly rich man. It is the desire of my heart to use a portion of my wealth as security for the protection of your valuable invention. Therefore, this is my proposition: in the event the Money Machine is stolen, destroyed, or expires due to wear that the passage of time brings, I will pay you the sum of 100,000 talents of gold to replace the loss of future income brought by any such misfortune."

I observed that Demas' eyes brightened and widened, as he thought that his faithful ears were deceiving him. "Such generosity, I have never before seen," he responded, as he gave me a big smile.

Then I told him, "You have not yet heard all of my proposition, for in return for that which you call generosity, I will require you to pay 500 gold talents to me each time the full moon appears. I will employ the gold you pay, so that it brings me much more of its own kind. If I am never required to make payment to you for loss, I will return all the gold talents you have paid for the protection I have provided, plus a reasonable profit. I will keep three gold talents out of every hundred I earn for you, in return for the protection and financial counsel that I provide. Now, my old friend, do you still call me generous?"

Demas thought momentarily, then answered, "Yes, I still call you generous. In fact, very generous! You have made me a proposition that I would be foolish to refuse. I humbly accept your most gracious offer."

The Money Machine produced enough of the precious metal to make Demas a very rich man. Numerous summers came and went and his fortune multiplied greatly. He religiously paid his 500 talents of gold to me at the appearance of every full moon. Many full moons passed with the swiftness of an eagle in flight, just as time flies for all men.

In the dead of the night, Demas was awakened by an unfamiliar noise coming from his laboratory. It was a rapid popping sound that was loud enough to startle him. Demas cautiously arose from his pallet and slipped on his robe as he made his way toward the noise. He entered the laboratory to discover the popping sound emitting from the Money Machine. There were some golden sparks shooting from the exterior openings of the device. He lit a candle to find that white smoke was filling the room. He hurried to the corner where the Money Machine sat on sturdy wooden legs. Suddenly, the popping sound ceased and then the shooting sparks and billowing smoke also stopped.

Demas immediately examined his valuable invention. He discovered that the tiny speck of Terrennium was missing from its chamber. After a thorough search and an examination of the residue he found in the chamber, he came to the disappointing conclusion that the mysterious material had ignited and then disintegrated. Evidently, the miracle matter had expended all of its energy and died. That event signaled the end of the Money Machine forever.

The alchemist reported the sad event to me. Upon being convinced that the unique device had indeed died, I paid Demas the 100,000 talents of gold in accordance with our agreement. He was pleased with the settlement, as was I, for he had paid me much gold to provide him protection against the possible loss of the future income. Thus ends the intriguing story of the Money Machine.

—m—

At this point, you may be wishing that you had a Money Machine of your own. My friend, I have good news, for you do have a money machine of your very own. Perhaps it can be even more valuable than Demas' if you will but keep it in the proper operating condition.

Hear me well: You, yourself, are the Money Machine. You have both the ability and opportunity to earn a fortune during your lifetime. See yourself, in your mind's eye, as a creation having unlimited power to build wealth. There is no other creature in existence exactly like you; you were uniquely formed in your mother's womb to make the very best of your God-given attributes, so that you may succeed in the service of others.

The future income stream that you are capable of earning will make you affluent, if it is managed properly. Therefore, you must realize that your potential earning power is a very valuable asset that must be protected against the possibility of loss, just as Demas arranged for the protection of the Money Machine through my willing assistance.

72

The adversaries that can steal away your future earning power and fortune are old age, sickness, disability, death, probate, taxes, and costly litigation in the courts of the land. Although it is possible to cope with every eventuality in life, any of these seven things bear the potential for significant financial loss.

The majority of young men starting out in life believe they will be successful and acquire their fair share of the world's wealth. They have big dreams and lofty aspirations. However, the truth of the matter is that only one out of every hundred becomes rich by the time he reaches his golden years when he truly needs money the most. Four out of every hundred achieve financial independence. Three must continue to work in order to meet their ongoing financial needs. Sixty-three will be dependent on family, friends, and charity just to have the necessities of life, and twenty-nine shall die prematurely somewhere along life's journey. Therefore, ninety-two out of every hundred are either dead or dead broke before they even reach their sunset years. Consequently, you must set a goal to be counted among the *top five percent* who realize financial freedom.

As a man journeys through life, he must face four critical financial challenges: wealth creation, wealth accumulation, wealth protection, and wealth conservation. The creation of wealth may be accomplished by rendering to your fellowman more and better service, which will bring you a continuously growing income. The accumulation of wealth may be attained by forming the habit of saving a minimum of one-tenth of all your income to employ and bring you more of its own kind. But the challenge of protecting and conserving your wealth will require thought and planning.

You may go to the great institutions that have many assets and abundant capital and specialize in helping people like yourself protect and conserve their wealth. Quality protection, at a reasonable cost, may be secured to prevent personal financial loss due to sickness, disability, death, or costly litigation. Protection may also be secured against the loss of your personal effects, chariots, carriages, and dwelling. My counsel is that you must secure your life, health, and possessions, so that if a thief should break in and steal any of these things, you and your loved ones will be adequately protected against economic loss.

Seek out experienced counselors who can help you develop a plan that will ensure your financial security and that of your family as well. Your plan should be your guide to accumulate, protect, and conserve your wealth. Such a plan should provide an uncontestable way to pass your estate to your loved ones without encountering costly probate expense and unnecessary taxes that would place a great financial burden on your heirs. Wise counselors can help you prepare a definitive financial plan that provides for every contingency of life.

In order to minimize the adverse consequences of old age, sickness, disability, death, litigation, probate, and taxes, your financial plan should accomplish the following:

I. Provide a proven method for accumulating wealth and a sound way to employ your money so that it will grow and bring you much more of its own kind

II. Provide protection against the loss of your future earning power due to sickness, disability, or death

III. Provide protection from economic loss due to litigation

IV. Provide protection against the loss of your material possessions due to accidents, disasters, and criminal acts

V. Provide relief from paying unnecessary taxes when you die, as well as throughout your life

VI. Provide deliverance from the excessive costs of probate when your estate is passed to your heirs

You, the Money Machine, must be wise, for you only get one chance to achieve a successful life. Hence, you must take full advantage of every minute, hour, day, and year that remains. You must

---

be prepared to grasp opportunities when they come. To do so, you must have a financial plan, for it is by design that a wise man acquires riches.

—⟋⟍—

An oracle to remember:

It takes a lifetime to build a great fortune that can be lost in the wink of an eye, unless proper planning and adequate protection are provided for the eventualities of life that can cause financial disaster.

VII

—∿—

*The man who practices pledging
his earthly possessions and
future earning power to
heartless money lenders is
indeed unwise, and will live
to regret his foolish ways.*

—∿—

THE SCROLL
NUMBERED SIX

—m—

Conquering Debt

Debt can be a very grievous evil for both mankind and nations. I am saddened to see the great number of people and governments that are under its merciless control. There is no end to the countless number of fools who come to financial ruin because of it.

Many irresponsible people who habitually abuse credit eventually become financially insolvent and seek the protection of the courts to deliver them from being accountable for their mistakes. They choose what appears to be an easy way out of a difficult situation by fleeing from their financial obligations under the shield of laws that were enacted solely for the purpose of helping unfortunate citizens who suffer great calamities. Ultimately, they discover their course of action to be unwise and the worst of all possible solutions, for the following reasons:

I. There are alternatives available that do not cause such great mental anguish, emotional stress, and expense. (I will share several of these alternatives with you in due course.)

II. In essence, they rob themselves of the priceless experience of working through their tribulation and gaining knowledge of paramount importance to future financial success. To rob themselves of such valuable learning is to ensure that they will one day repeat their folly. However, those who are courageous enough to endure such a difficult experience become enlightened, learn prudence, and understand the mysterious ways of money.

III. Building an honorable reputation takes a lifetime, but a good name can be destroyed in an instant in the courts of the land. Choosing the protection of the courts to escape the responsibility for irresponsible financial actions marks a man for life. If a man possesses genuine character, he will not attempt to deliberately pursue a course of action in troubled financial times that will ill-treat his creditors and set him free from his obligation to pay what he ethically owes. A man of real character will go to any lengths to protect and preserve his honor as well as the respect of his fellowman.

My counsel to you is that if you have already sought protection from the obligation to pay your just debts, do everything possible to rectify the situation with every person whom you owe. What is done is done! The consequences you suffer due to your former actions cannot be reversed nor changed. However, it is possible for you to minimize the adverse effects by going to each of your creditors and attempting to set the record straight. Stop at nothing in order to make amends and restore your good name.

Never shun the payment of your debts, for such folly would prevent you from ever becoming rich. Honesty is a prerequisite of the abundant life. A good name is of greater value than gold. When you borrow, repay, for your word is your bond. If you should act otherwise, the abundant life will elude you.

For much of my life, I have had the privilege of counseling many men who were overcome by financial difficulties. Without exception I discovered that, although their situation was serious, it was not hopeless. Now I will reveal to you, just as I revealed to them, a

80

proven way that, if applied, will take you out of the abyss of financial despair and point you in the direction of untold riches. However, you should constantly be reminded that it takes a significant amount of time to sink to the bottom of the pit of economic crisis and, therefore, will also require adequate time to resolve the crisis and attain financial freedom. You must realize that a permanent solution will entail a process instead of an instant remedy. But as sure as the sun sets on the western horizon, the experience you will gain from seeing the process through to fulfillment shall greatly add to your fortune.

There are several ways that you must prepare yourself in order to conquer debt:

I. Develop a strong aversion to owing money to anyone. Learn to hate debt just as you hate the Devil himself. Train your mind's eye to see debt as a formidable adversary that seeks to destroy your life and enslave you indefinitely.

II. Resolve to forego the mistakes of youthful self-indulgences and rely solely on the time-tested profound knowledge known as *wisdom*. A good rule of thumb is never—no never—spend money before you have it in your possession. Many times you will be tempted to spend more than you earn and thus sow seeds of thoughtless self-indulgence, which grow into a harvest of financial troubles, mortification, and disgrace. You must not yield to such threatening temptations.

Decide what is genuinely important in life. Is it the immediate gratification of the fleeting desires of a weak moment, such as costly jewelry, expensive raiment, fine wine, or exotic food that are soon forgotten? Or is it possessions having permanent value such as a comfortable dwelling, quality furnishings, land, savings, and income-bearing investments that provide a lifetime of satisfaction? The money you spend unwisely purchases the first, but the money you keep and employ will bring you the latter. Which is most important to you?

Hopefully, you wisely chose the latter. Do not abandon your conviction in either good times or bad, for you will face both throughout your life. Resolve to live by sound financial principles, for they will never forsake you and will guide you on your journey to riches.

III.   You must constantly be vigilant so that you do not succumb to the enticement of easy credit, for this could well be the beginning of many financial woes. Do not feel disheartened if you have already succumbed to the allure of easy credit, for you are not alone in your folly. Multitudes have made the same mistake, becoming innocent captives, just like a fly becomes snared in the sprawling web of a ravenous spider.

The borrower is the servant of the lender. When a borrower is foolish enough to extend his credit so far that he cannot pay, he must face consequences dictated by a heartless money lender, which is a sore experience that he shall never forget.

No individual or nation can survive indefinitely if the unsound practice of thriving on borrowed money is the order of things. There shall be a day of reckoning just as sure as the seasons come and go, for the *Principles of the Harvest* are unfailing: seeds that are sown must come to harvest in full measure. Debt is an agent of financial calamity that will not be denied realization. Debt can bring down the mighty and meek alike. Therefore, both men and nations would be wise to refrain from depending on its use.

At this point, I will share with you three important tenets that, if religiously followed, will transform the unpleasantness of burdensome debt into a blessing of financial strength and freedom.

Tenet I

The philosophy of wise men regarding personal indebtedness

Money is the god of this world and money lenders the prophets. The enticements of the money lenders are so appealing that they possess the power to lure many who are naive into the worst sort of bondage. It is indeed an empty purse that is filled with borrowed money.

In essence, the use of credit is neither good nor bad, for that determination is made by the borrower. When properly understood, controlled, and managed, credit can serve a salutary economic purpose. When misunderstood and misused, however, credit can bring all manner of troubles. Troubles so great, they make the nights sleepless and the days filled with discouragement and despair.

While the use of credit should not be forbidden to the wise who manage their financial affairs properly, self-imposed prohibition must be practiced by those who have an affinity for borrowing and misusing money. You must honestly evaluate your own personal attributes and, if such a weakness exists, act accordingly.

If you borrow, employ credit wisely, and never enter into a pledge with a lender if wickedly usurious rates are charged as a condition for granting the pledge. Seek and acquire equitable rates and therefore avoid excessive rates, for wisdom dictates that wickedly usurious rates grow incessantly without the benefit of rainfall. Wickedly usurious rates are like the bite of a viper who looks small, but whose poison is deadly.

Tenet II

How to permanently escape the bondage of debt

Extreme indebtedness is a condition that usually results from the abuse of credit over a long period of time. Therefore, if you are a debtor you must face the reality that it will require a lengthy term to effect a cure that will permanently heal the condition. You must willingly resolve to stay the course until you are set free from the financial slavery to which you subject yourself. Your faith will one day be rewarded and you will find that achieving freedom from debt was worth every sacrifice that you made. The greatest reward comes from that for which the greatest price is paid.

There are certain individual characteristics found in a man who falls victim to the weakness of employing credit unwisely:

I. He may suffer from a habitual debt syndrome that he learned from his parents.

II. He may have developed an obsession for self-gratification so strong that when carried to the extreme, it becomes extravagance.

III. He may be the victim of his own naivety.

IV. He may not have the benefit of an effective and reliable financial plan.

If you earnestly desire to free yourself from the slavery of debt, first determine which of your personal characteristics is responsible for your dilemma. Once this determination is made, you should act immediately to reform your shortcoming.

There are certain reasons why a man prone to living under the weightiness of debt first descends into such a pit of agonizing torment:

I. He lacks the personal discipline to forego his inner urge to impulsively purchase all manner of possessions that he does not have the means to pay for. Impulse buying thus proves to be his ever-present nemesis.

II. He subscribes to a mentality that makes him vulnerable to participation in get-rich-quick schemes through the use of credit.

III. He has an insatiable appetite for pleasure, status, and luxury, which he constantly feeds with borrowed money and which ultimately leads to embarrassment, insolvency, and ruin.

IV. He fails to develop and follow any sort of sensible financial plan, thus leaving himself open to the dangers of folly.

84

If you have knowingly or unknowingly fallen over the precipice of debt, immediately catch hold of a protruding rock to stop your descent and then climb back up to financial security. The struggle shall be difficult, but the priceless reward will be worth the effort.

Essentially, there are two separate types of debt that tend to become the source of a debt addict's woes. *Secured debt* is the kind a man creates by pledging possessions such as a dwelling or land as collateral to be held by a money lender to secure the repayment of the indebtedness. If the debtor fails to pay, the money lender keeps the collateral, which is usually worth more than the amount owed. *Unsecured debt* is the kind that does not require a pledge of collateral by the debtor because the amount borrowed is normally small. The danger of the availability of unsecured debt is that a debt addict will use numerous money lenders to borrow small sums which all equate to a large sum on which the borrower pays inordinate usury rates. Either of these types of debt becomes an instrument of financial catastrophe when used irresponsibly. You have ears to hear, so hear this warning well.

All is not lost if you find yourself caught in the midst of tormenting debt that you do not have the money to repay. There is a proven way to restore financial stability and protect your good name:

I. You must first face the reality of your situation and resolve that the repayment of your debt is both a moral and legal responsibility, and that the repudiation of your debt is not a viable solution.

II. You should consider the idea of debt consolidation only as a last resort, because the risk of repeating your folly would simply compound your problems, and your irresponsible spending habits would still remain.

III. You must make an accurate evaluation of your financial affairs in writing, which will serve as your resource for a new plan for the future.

IV. You must devise a plan, in writing, designed to incrementally retire your debt and set you on a new course toward financial solvency. The elements of your plan should include the following:

- A firm resolution that you will follow your plan and become debt free, placing strong emphasis on the discontinuance of your senseless spending.
- A calculation of your actual spendable income, which represents the amount of income that remains after an accurate allocation for taxes is made and a gift of one-tenth of your income to charity is deducted.
- An allocation of your spendable income divided thusly:
  —Keep one-tenth for yourself that you should employ to bring you more of its own kind
  —Provide seven-tenths for the care of your family and the maintenance of your household
  —Pay two-tenths to your creditors regularly, until your debt is eventually eliminated
- The preceding guidelines may be adapted to circumstances that warrant different payment allocations.

V. Face each of your creditors privately and explain your financial crisis with complete honesty, as well as your plan for the repayment of the debt. The amount you pay to each creditor should be in proportion to the amount owed. Assure your creditors that you fully intend to meet your obligation. Seek the blessing of your creditors, but do not be disheartened if you fail to gain their full support, for with or without their blessing, you must see your plan to fruition.

By accepting responsibility for the timely payment of debt, you display the essential qualities found in genuinely successful men who procure great wealth, for honesty is a virtue that is blessed by the Lord. The *rewards* for your commitment are *wisdom* gained through trial, *self-esteem* acquired through accomplishment, *respect* earned through trustworthiness, *fulfillment* attained through perseverance, *happiness* fostered through contentment, and *freedom* from the slavery of debt realized through tenacity.

Tenet III

The philosophy of wise men regarding borrowing

A wise man refrains from borrowing funds to satisfy his personal indiscretions, but if legitimate circumstances arise that require him to borrow, there are certain guidelines he follows to avoid financial misfortune. If you are to borrow money, follow them.

I. Control your weakness for making expensive impulsive purchases by writing down the name of the item you desire and then vowing not to purchase it until thirty days have passed. You will find that with the passage of time, your desire for the item subsides and its purchase shall no longer be of importance. However, if you still have genuine desire for the item, you should then seriously consider its purchase if you can pay. Under no circumstances borrow a large sum at exceedingly usurious rates for the purpose of purchasing an item that quickly depreciates in value. The purchase of such an item should be made with cash, if made at all.

II. Ill-fortune will be your lot if you think more of borrowing than repaying. When debt becomes necessary, it is not prohibited. However, exercise extreme caution regarding the terms of the pledge to the lender. Under favorable circumstances, the use of debt may be advisable if it is procured wisely for a wise purpose.

III. If debt is necessary, do not borrow from your relatives, friends, or employer. The best intention to repay can go amok due to unforeseen difficulties that are beyond your ability to control. Such difficulties can cause much heartache, division, and bitterness. Borrowing is simply not worth the risk of important broken relationships.

IV. Avoid borrowing from seedy money lenders who employ questionable practices and charge usurious rates.

V. Charge nothing on easy credit that you do not have the money to pay for after the passage of no more than thirty sunrises.

VI. Do not give surety to a money lender under any circumstances, especially when it involves monetary transactions with strangers. Assuming the responsibility for the debt of another is indeed foolish and many times leads to sore troubles.

VII. Do not accumulate long-term debt. Plan your financial affairs in such a manner that, in time, you will have no debt for a duration longer than seven years. The collateral value of such debt should be great enough to repay the money lender if unforeseen misfortune should rear its ugly head.

VIII. Before you elect to acquire debt, devise a plan to repay. If you cannot repay, you should forego acquiring debt.

You will be wise to follow the teaching of the sixth scroll, for you shall know freedom from debt and avoid the misfortune that debt can bring. May you enjoy good health and live a long and successful life, for freedom from debt is the freedom to live.

—m—

An oracle to remember:

Learn to live life free from the ill effects of enslaving debt, for financial liability and financial independence are not compatible bedfellows.

VIII

—◊—

Self is an
impossible god
to serve.

—◊—

THE SCROLL
NUMBERED SEVEN

—ᨏ—

Blessed Giving

That a man can give of his fortune to help others and yet have more is indeed a paradox. This makes no sense to the worldly individual who is ensnared by materialism, for it defies human logic. The perception of a worldly individual is confined to worldly matters and, therefore, cannot relate to higher law of a spiritual nature. However, this concept makes a great deal of sense to the spiritual person who accepts and comprehends higher law. To such a person, the maxim "It is more blessed to give than to receive" means much more than the simple beauty of poetic words. It defines an unwritten law that makes the world a better place in which to live and brings both spiritual and material blessings to the one who gives.

God dearly loves a cheerful giver who makes giving a habit. The Lord will see to it that all his needs are met. Therefore, he will have ample funds to give. Faithful giving represents seeds planted for future harvests. You cannot give more than God will give to you in return. God faithfully rewards all who manage their financial affairs in accordance with His guidelines concerning giving.

In order to achieve financial freedom by following God's financial guidelines, you must make certain destiny-changing commitments:

I. Commit yourself to honor the Lord with your life, which will give your existence profound meaning and purpose. Spiritual enlightenment contributes to good character, which is the cornerstone of true riches. No amount of wealth can set you free to live your fullest and atone for poverty of character. Only through a meaningful relationship with your Maker can you accomplish these things.

II. Commit yourself to honor the Lord with your wealth, for your Creator is the eternal proprietor of everything that exists, property and wealth included. The best way for you to honor the Most High is with your wealth, for your heartstring is attached securely to your pursestring. The Almighty will test the sincerity of your heart with the challenge of sharing your finances with others who are in need. Nothing reveals your true character as much as the uses to which you put your money.

III. Commit yourself to honor the Lord by discovering why your Maker supplies you with more money than is required to meet your own financial necessities. You have more so that you may give more, and you will receive more, that you may then give again. Joyfully give a generous portion of all you earn and find much favor with the Great Provider.

To become wise regarding financial matters is an immeasurable blessing. Wisdom is essential to the attainment of the abundant life. Therefore, I will share with you the *Miracle of the Faith-Harvest,* a compilation of laws that a man destined to become prosperous must learn. So, hear me well.

The First Law

You will faithfully look to God as the sole source of supply for your daily sustenance.

The treasury of the Almighty is filled with infinite riches that He is pleased to share liberally with those who love and honor Him with the first portion of their financial harvests. The omnipotent Ruler of heaven and earth is the only unlimited source of supply that exists. All other sources—yourself, relatives, friends, employers, and government—have perplexing limitations because they are finite in origin. There is nothing on earth to compare to the opulence of the Lord, so be quick to seek His favor for your livelihood, for He alone is worthy of complete trust regarding your destiny.

Once there was a grower of figs who had many abundant harvests. One season, however, adversity struck like a bolt of lightning. As the tiny figs appeared on the tree branches, locusts came in such great numbers that they covered the earth for as far as his eyes could see. No growing thing in their destructive path survived without serious damage. The once flourishing fig trees that lined his groves were totally ravaged. Nothing survived except for the trees themselves, which were stripped bare of their foliage and fruit. The immense devastation was a discouraging sight that the grower would never forget. He was the victim of a calamity over which he had no control. He had watched, helplessly, as his groves were destroyed, leaving him in despair.

Through this adversity, the grower learned a great lesson. He had always assumed that his source of sustenance came from the large, plump figs that he grew so bountifully, for they were food for his table and were sold for a top price at the market. The gold they brought filled his purse. The plague of locusts taught him that it was not the figs, but instead the fig trees, from which his livelihood grew. So, from that day forth, he nurtured his fig trees more carefully than ever, for they would again bud, grow, ripen, and yield many future harvests.

The parable of the grower may be likened unto a man who puts all his faith in finite sources for his sustenance when the only infinite source of supply worthy of his trust is God. Do not place limitations on God's ability to meet your needs by seeking other sources for your livelihood. Do not rely on the promise of this imperfect world for your sustenance; only the Lord's blessings have genuine significance and permanence.

The Second Law

Faithfully give from all you earn, so that what you give may be perpetually returned to you in inexhaustible amounts.

Giving must become a priority of life, as much so as slumber, food, and drink. Giving must become a habit. Be quick to give from your means to needy orphans, the poor, the aged, the homeless, the hungry, the sick, the handicapped, and those upon whom disaster falls.

The most blessed form of giving is to help your fellowman help himself. The next most blessed way is to help those in need anonymously and secretly, not knowing who the recipients of your charity are, so that they will feel no obligation to repay you. You may also assist the poor and the needy to earn a living that permits them to maintain their self-respect and dignity. At all cost, the poor and the needy must be spared embarrassment.

The man who has an adequate income, but refuses to live within his means and yet seeks the support of charity, should not be helped. Such a man should be left to endure the consequences of his own folly, so that he may learn his lesson. Help a man such as this with your counsel and love, but do not support him financially for you will then become a contributor to his delusion.

The man who has a sound mind and a strong back and yet refuses to work should not be helped, except for caring for him and giving him wise counsel. Such a man should not eat. To feed him regularly from your table is to approvingly acknowledge his slothful lifestyle. For his own benefit, leave such a man to experience the harsh reality that life will teach him.

Avoid pernicious gifts to false religions, people who practice evil instead of good, causes contrary to the teachings of God, and foul schemes conceived through greed. Be most particular about where your charity goes and whom it helps. Choose carefully, relying on the guidance of the Sacred Writings and much thought and prayer before committing your gifts to any individual or purpose.

Giving should know neither color nor race, for every man needs to learn of his Maker's generosity and love. People of the world are as hungry for the knowledge of God as they are for food to fill their bellies. In truth, many suffer from spiritual famine.

If a man in genuine need asks for financial assistance and you have no money to give him, then give him love, hope, and encouragement. Giving of yourself to him is a profound act of charity, equally as important as sharing your finances. In the eternal scheme of things, you are measured by what you do in relation to what you have. Give to match your income, lest God makes your income to match your gifts. The heart, not the gift, makes the true giver.

The character of the giver is of utmost importance. Do not give simply to receive in return, for God will not honor an attitude of greed. Let your giving originate from a pure heart. This concept makes little sense to men of the world whose only goal in life is to heap up riches.

At this point, it is important that I tell you about the dynamics of *seed-giving*. You will receive in proportion and in kind what you have planted, for the certainty of your reward is ensured by the *Principles of the Harvest*. Giving may be likened unto planting seeds in God's garden. God nurtures them. God multiplies them. God makes them fruitful. God brings forth an abundant harvest. God Himself, being the gardener, will see to it that your yield is plentiful.

There are certain guidelines you should follow in order to ensure the Lord's blessing over your seed-gifts of money:

I. Plant your seed-gifts with a joyous attitude, expecting nothing in return. Plant them willingly, not grudgingly.

II. Plant no less than one-tenth of your gross earnings to promote God's work in the world. Observe how your seed-gifts multiply and return to you in full measure.

III. Plant more as your prosperity increases, the amount of which should be determined by the conviction of your heart as it silently listens to the leading of the Lord. The willingness to plant more of your growing surplus is a test of your character, for it demonstrates that you possess a greater love for God than for money.

The Almighty never permits His work among men to go undone due to the lack of financial resources. He sees to it that people who love Him and have a heart for giving receive abundantly, so that they may give abundantly. In essence, this explains the dynamics of seed-giving.

The Third Law

Joyously give, believing with unwavering faith that God will honor your gifts by prospering you proportionately, just as He has promised in the Sacred Writings.

Just as the farmer sows grains of wheat with the expectation that they will grow and yield a bountiful harvest, you must expect your seed-gifts to grow and bring more into your purse so that you may continue to give more. To expect God to be true to His promise is an act of faith that finds great favor with Him. He is pleased to bless those who exhibit their belief in the faith-harvest by practicing seed-giving and, therefore, returns to them many bumper crops. Expect a bountiful faith-harvest. To do so is an obvious demonstration of your faith and gives evidence to others that you trust God to take the faith-seeds you plant, make them prolific, and continuously yield abundant faith-harvests.

The Lord does not ask you to plant more seeds than you have, requiring you to give more than you have to give. But He does expect you to plant from the seeds you possess by giving from the money that regularly fills your purse. The Lord loves a generous, cheerful giver.

Heed the example set by the farmer: plant first, then harvest. You must plant your faith-seeds before it becomes possible to receive a faith-harvest. Plant abundantly and you will reap exceedingly abundantly. Be faithful and diligent with your seed-gifts and watch the hand of the Lord at work in all that you do. Hear me well: give from a pure heart and you will one day understand the limitless power of the axiom, "It is more blessed to give than to receive."

—ᴍ—

An oracle to remember:

If you give joyfully and liberally from your purse,
so that all men everywhere may have the opportunity
to know God and the truly needy may have their needs
met, you will never suffer from lack and your purse will
be continuously refilled to overflowing.

—ᴍ—

I, a man of great wealth, have experienced everything that my soul has desired. I have arrived at several conclusions concerning wealth. By definition, the word "wealth" means different things to different people. To some, it means great riches. To others, it means having enough money to purchase numerous things and yet live from hand to mouth. To a few who are wise, it means seeking and finding the abundant life and thus gaining everything worthwhile that life has to offer. I discovered the latter to be the epitome of true riches.

My search of the Sacred Writings revealed that the body, soul, and spirit constitute the essence of man's being—body, soul, and spirit being synonymous with the physical, mental, and spiritual realms of existence. Each is intertwined with the other making them one, like a triple-braided cord.

Materialism appeals only to the physical and mental instincts of man. Without the interweaving of all three realms of existence, man is no more than a highly evolved animal species. Men who are driven strictly by the allure of materialism live an imbalanced life and thus attract every sort of malady. Dissatisfaction and unhappiness are their lot. Material possessions do not bring peace of mind. At best, they bring only temporary enjoyment. Lasting fulfillment is the reward of living a balanced life.

You would be unwise to seek money simply for money's sake. If you do so, you will live to rue the day it came to you for it shall be a weighty burden instead of the heavenly blessing that it could be. In your quest to build wealth, seek within and find the three dimensions of your being. Nurture each of these dimensions with care, uniting them into a single worthy purpose for acquiring wealth, and it will come to you surely, bringing with it many blessed benefits.

The essence of man is a composite of body, soul, and spirit. The body instinctively seeks to meet physical needs such as food, water, survival, and copulation that support procreation and life. The soul, the mental dimension of man, is occupied with learning, courage, possessions, status, popularity, titles, fame, money, and power. The spirit, which is the quintessential part of man's three dimensions, holds the potential for a relationship with God, and consists of love, joy, peace, patience, kindness, goodness, faithfulness, gentleness, and self-control. Knowing this, you can clearly understand how an imbalance in any of these three dimensions results in abnormal human behavior.

Before you seek anything else, seek righteousness and the kingdom of God. All the worthwhile things you yearn for will be within your reach. Herein lies the secret of the abundant life. A wise man soon learns that a spiritual man has the capacity to develop both body and soul, so that the whole being thrives in harmony. Balance is essential to skillful, abundant living.

Begin to observe the natural abundance that surrounds you in everyday life. See the lush green valleys, snow-capped mountains, tall forests, rambling rivers, blue seas, sandy beaches, broad prairies, vast deserts, and majestic heavens. There are no limits to what the Creator has provided.

In the material world, notice the enchanting temples, magnificent palaces, bustling cities, thriving businesses, and bounteous affluence. There appears to be no end to what man can accomplish.

There is so much abundance that it makes the eyes weary just trying to see it all. Hear me well: you have as much right to earn your share of that abundance as any other person. Riches are not reserved for an elite class who are luckier or smarter than you. They are reserved exclusively for those individuals who will to have them. Prosperity beckons you to earn your rightful share. Be aware that the outcome does not depend on outside circumstances or anyone other than yourself. This precept may sound too good to be true, but you may rest assured that it is profoundly true.

Enduring wealth cannot come to you until you have prepared yourself to receive it. Such truth exists because mankind is subject to the *Law of Cause and Effect*. For every action, there is a reaction. Action, or cause, is the visible manifestation of thought. Thought is the invisible energy that makes and molds the material environment in which you live. You are where you are because of the pattern of your past thoughts. Your future is shaped by the pattern of your present thoughts. Unquestionably, thoughts become things and the man who is intelligent enough to integrate godliness with wealth demonstrates human nature in its finest hour.

Charity, luck, and fate are poor companions that tend to enslave the thoughts of everyone who perpetually turns to them for a helping hand. In reality, they are but subtle adversaries that prevent man from ever rising above his exiguous circumstances. No man can climb to the top of the economic ladder if he elects to dwell permanently under their debilitating power. To think otherwise is pure self-deception. Resolve to rise above the tantalizing temptation to avail yourself to the enticement of these three spellbinding seductresses, or you will suffer wretched misfortune all your days.

The thought-life makes or breaks an individual. Thoughts are the seeds of actions and actions create circumstances. If you truly desire to change your circumstances, you must first alter your thoughts. Consequently, if you want to be rich, your thoughts must focus on the means to your end. In essence, you must temporarily exist under the circumstances of your current condition, but you must think in terms of acquiring wealth and little by little you will exchange lack for plenty until your thoughts of riches materialize.

A man is tossed and buffeted by circumstances as long as he thinks himself to be a creature whose life is shaped and molded by outside conditions. When he comes to the realization that he is a creative power that can command and control the hidden resources within, out of which circumstances grow, he will become the master of his destiny. Yes, you may change the circumstances of your life at your command. In fact, you may do so several times during your sojourn on earth as many do, but you can never change your circumstances even one iota unless you first will it so through the mastery of your thoughts.

Welfare regularly and gratuitously doled out to the same able-bodied men is a grievous evil regardless of the benevolent purpose intended. It robs its recipients of their independence, dignity, and self-worth and permanently enslaves them to a life of dependence, limitation, and want. Welfare is the worst possible bondage. Encourage men who are capable of work to work and develop their God-given potential, so that they may become happy, self-reliant, and fulfilled. A government that enslaves people in welfare seeks to further the interests of those who rule and possesses no real concern for the genuine well-being of the populace. Flee from any entanglement that promises something for nothing, for such practices violate the universal law of effort and reward and thus will eventually become a giant millstone tied about your neck.

The difference in the economic status of men is due solely to the difference in the substance of their thoughts. Intelligence and academic excellence are worthy attributes, but they are not essential to financial success. Principled thoughts, aptly directed, lift men up to attain *true* riches.

Begin your ascent to riches by first looking within to discover the way and then transform your vision into a mentality that cultivates wealth. This inner transformation gives rise to ideas, goals, plans, courage, desire, and unrelenting persistence. When you initiate bona fide change from within, your material world responds compliantly and changes from without. Thus you find riches because you become a new person, transformed in both thoughts and actions. The cause that originates in your thoughts results in an effect that manifests itself in your material world.

There is nothing wrong with wanting to be rich. However, there is something wrong if riches are pursued for the wrong reasons and in the wrong manner. After all, what real profit is there for a man who gains the whole world if, in the process, he forfeits himself? The ultimate reward for lust, greed, and envy is destruction. There is but one way to acquire *true* riches, and that way requires the development of body, soul, and spirit—the whole man.

Here is the final piece of advice given to you from a man who has lived as a king and done everything that his soul desired: love God and follow his teachings, be happy, work hard, give service, exercise prudence, show generosity, enjoy living, flee iniquity, embrace virtue, love others just as you love yourself, and you will delight in the abundant life all your days. Remember, it is far better to live rich than to die rich.

IX

—⚬—

Every man is a miracle!
Hidden deep within his bosom
is something special waiting to
surface and grow into a great
work. Honor a man for what
is hidden within, for once
discovered, that he
will become.

—⚬—

BUILDING
WEALTH

—m—

F inally, Andy finished reading the seven scrolls. He simply sat in the big overstuffed chair as a sensation of awe overwhelmed yet inspired him. What he had just finished reading had much greater value than the extraordinary price the golden scrolls would have brought. On his lap lay a stack of papers that revealed the secrets of building wealth, given to him by one of the wisest and richest men who ever lived. What more could an ambitious young man hope for?

He wanted to read the scrolls again, which he did. Then again. All told, he read them once each day for the next thirty days. He studied and learned the important principles they taught. He memorized the seven oracles and could repeat them at will. He persevered until he achieved conscious mastery over every important detail.

The profound knowledge he gained gave him enthusiasm and self-confidence. He had changed—changed permanently and for the better. This change would eventually guide him to prodigious riches and success.

Andy reasoned that he should begin his ascent up the economic ladder by establishing goals and making detailed plans for their accomplishment. To synopsize, this is what he did:

First, from the night table next to his bed he picked up a Bible that had been presented to him years before by his parents. He turned to a passage in Psalms he had discovered while in the En-gedi wilderness that says, "Be delighted with the Lord. Then He will give you all your hearts desires. Commit everything you do to the Lord. Trust Him to help you do it and He will." He closed the Bible and put it back on the night table. Then he got down on his knees beside his bed, clasped his hands together in front of him, bowed his head, and whispered, "Lord, this is Andy. I place my life and future in your hands. I will follow where you lead, always doing your will, so that you may be honored before men through my example. I will work hard and do my part, but I will trust you for the outcome of my success. Amen."

Second, he took a pencil and writing pad from the dresser top, sat down on the side of his bed, and wrote:

My Goals for Building Wealth

1. Measure every decision by the standards of the Holy Scriptures.

2. Study the Holy Scriptures to learn about skillful living and success.

3. Form the habit of praying and seeking God's guidance about everything.

4. Seek employment in the path of opportunity and growth.

5. Render more and better service than my competition.

6. Eliminate my personal debts within the next 24 months.

7. Save a minimum of one-tenth of all that I earn.

8. Give a minimum of one-tenth of all that I earn.

9. Seek wise counsel regarding the best way to invest my savings.

10. Take the right steps to protect my future earning power.

11. Show proper respect for money, so that I may manage it wisely.

12. Follow a detailed budgetary plan all the days of my life.

Andy spent two weeks working on a comprehensive plan of action for implementing each of his goals. When he finished, he felt powerful and committed. His enthusiasm was evident. Little did he realize that he was experiencing the first stage of a transformation that would change his life forever.

Fortunately, he found himself in the path of progress while working as a clerk for a major railroad company in the East. The superintendent of the railroad had discovered Andy's potential while he worked as a messenger boy, then telegrapher for the local telegraph company at a meager salary.

This particular railroad wanted to set up its own telegraph system and Andy was made superintendent of the new telegraph department. His beginning salary was more than $30 per month, which was soon increased to $40 due to his exceptional performance.

Andy was a clean, hard-working young man who knew nothing base or vile. Ironically, he was cast into the midst of hard, vulgar men who held positions as engineers, freight conductors, brakemen, and firemen. He was accepted and well liked, but he never found himself wanting to partake of their ways. He was good at his job and they respected him for it.

The superintendent of the railroad became very fond of Andy because he was industrious. One day, the superintendent asked his youthful protege if he had any money. If so, the superintendent told him, he would like for him to purchase several shares of a new stock issue offered by an upstart communications company. Andy scrimped and saved and eventually came up with the needed amount. This was the first of many investments of this kind he would make over the course of his lifetime. The first monthly dividend he received was impressive. The young Scotsman truly felt that he had found the goose that lays golden eggs.

In those days, America was a frothing pot of growth and expansion. The West was beckoning and the railroads were the means of answering the call. They were a pathway to opportunity and Andy was on the right path.

The young Scotsman displayed initiative. He took it upon himself to make difficult corporate decisions in the absence of the superintendent of the railroad. He was responsible for negotiating a satisfactory settlement of a labor strike, which gained him much favor with his superior. He was eager and willing, and he never permitted obstacles to stand in his way. Eight-hour work days were for others with less ambition; he simply worked until his objectives were completed, regardless of the number of hours it took.

On one of his assignments he met the man who invented the sleeping car, which eventually became a major innovation in long-range railroad travel. Andy helped the inventor sell his idea to the railroad company. In deep gratitude, the inventor asked Andy to join him in his venture by offering the wide-eyed Scot an eighth interest. He quickly accepted the proposition and scraped together the investment capital he needed. This resulted in the first serious money he made from investments.

His accomplishments soon gained him a promotion to Division Superintendent at an annual salary of $1,500. Along with the outbreak of the Civil War, his boss and mentor was called to Washington to serve as Assistant Secretary of War. Consequently, Andy was summoned to assist him. Andy was placed in charge of the military railroad system and telegraph operations for the government. He sometimes worked at the side of the president himself, for whom he had much admiration and respect.

As the conflict gradually worsened, the war had no end in sight. Thus, Andy's boss could no longer be spared from the railroad company and was reassigned to his former job to bolster railway transportation for the war effort. As a result, Andy returned to his railroad duties in Pittsburgh where his services were badly needed due to the increased demands on transportation that the war had brought.

The Civil War created a huge demand for iron from which the instruments of battle were forged. However, this demand caused a shortage of train rails. The energetic Scotsman immediately put together a group of partners and raised enough investment capital to form a company that would make rails. He organized another company to manufacture locomotives, which were also in great demand. Shortly after the turn of the century, shares of this company originally purchased for $100 sold for $3,000.

Due to the war and westward expansion, the railroad companies needed iron bridges to cross great rivers such as the Ohio and the Mississippi. Therefore, Andy organized a company to build iron bridges, in which he invested little more than $1,200 for a one-fifth interest. The age of iron had come in America and the young Scot took full advantage of the opportunity.

The oil industry was growing so Andy invested in oil wells in Pennsylvania. Eventually, his investments began requiring so much of his time that he resigned from his position with the railroad company. He later said, "I was determined to make my fortune. It became clear to me that I could not reach this goal while working for the railroad." That was the last time he ever worked for a salary.

During his rise from poverty to riches, he was careful to remain focused on his goals and he followed his plan of action to the letter. From time to time during his ascent, it became necessary to revise his goals and plans, but never once did he abandon them. He remained true to the course he had written down while sitting on the side of his bed in the rooming house years before.

Andy read and reread the seven scrolls so many times during those years that the paper on which they were written grew soiled and worn. So much so, he took them to a print shop and had them copied and bound into a book for his personal use. Throughout those years he kept a poster-size rendering of the seven oracles on his office wall where he could read them each day. When he was once asked about the oracles by a business associate he replied, "They are the beacon that lights my pathway to prosperity."

The end of the Civil War resulted in a national commitment to rebuild an America that was independent from European influence. Capital for manufacturing became abundant. Free trade was established with European countries. Opportunity abounded.

The iron age passed into the age of steel. Remaining true to his commitment to always position himself in the path of progress, Andy organized a mill operation to make Bessemer steel. He later established other steel plants. His holdings in steel mills and related industries became one of the greatest industrial enterprises in America.

Andy's accomplishments became the talk of the New York financial establishment. His extraordinary exploits were even acknowledged abroad. Consequently, a New York financier made him a proposition to purchase his railroad interests, and he could not refuse. Therefore, he sold at a most attractive price.

When in his early thirties, he capped his personal earnings at $50,000 per year. At that point he began giving all of his surplus income to benevolent causes. He once said, "Man has created many kinds of idols and the worst of them is wealth. The worship of money is both debasing and evil." This was a philosophy that he lived by throughout his life.

Andy's holdings in the steel industry grew copiously. His achievements were far beyond his original expectations. He gave credit to the veracity of the *Principles of the Harvest* for his extraordinary success, as well as the *Miracle of the Faith-Harvest* for the creation of abundant surplus. When his profits reached $40 million per year, he decided to cease building wealth and concentrate on using his wealth to help others. The message of the golden scrolls had taught him that God sends thread for a web that is begun.

All told, Andy gave away over $350 million to worthy causes during his lifetime. He endowed numerous foundations to aid his former workers, public libraries, museums, veterans, schools, teachers, research, the aged, the poverty stricken, and churches. It is doubtful that any other person in history has given as much money to the benefit of mankind.

The same New York financier who had purchased his railroad interests eventually purchased his steel holdings also. This transaction freed him to spend the rest of his life giving away his fortune. By the time he died, he had succeeded in achieving his goal.

A former Secretary of State said of him, "He belonged to that great race of nation-builders who have made the development of America the wonder of the world. . . . He was the kindliest man I ever knew. Wealth had brought him no hardening of the heart, nor made him forget the dreams of his youth. Kindly, affectionate, charitable in his judgments, unrestrained in his sympathies, noble in his impulses, I wish that all the people who think of him as a rich man giving away money he did not need could know of the hundreds of kindly things he did unknown to the world."

He emerged from rough beginnings to conquer the world of business. His interest in literature and art has left a legacy that Americans shall enjoy for centuries. He, himself, wrote several books, one of which shared many of the financial precepts he had learned from the seven scrolls.

Andy's single most important and valuable relationship existed for a short time at the beginning of the Civil War when he had worked side by side with President Lincoln. Andy said of him, "All the pictures of this extraordinary man are like him. He was so marked of feature that it was impossible for anyone to paint him and not produce a likeness. He was certainly one of the most homely men I ever saw when his features were in repose; but when excited or telling a story, intellect shone through his eyes and illuminated his face to a degree that I have seldom or never seen in any other person. His manners were perfect because they were natural, and he had a kind word for everybody, even the youngest boy in the office. They were the same to all, as deferential in talking to the messenger boy as to Secretary Seward. His charm lay in the total absence of manner. It was not so much, perhaps, what he said as the way in which he said it that never failed to win someone over. I have often regretted that I did not note down carefully at the time some of his curious sayings, for he said even common things in an original way. I never met a great man who so thoroughly made himself one with all men as Mr. Lincoln. As Secretary Hay so well says, 'It is impossible to imagine anyone a valet to Mr. Lincoln; he would have been his companion.' He was the most perfect democrat, revealing in every word and act the equality of men."

Andy's love and adoration for the President was immense. The great Lincoln had ten guidelines by which he lived and governed that had a profound effect on Andy's life. So much so, that he adopted them for his own. He followed these guidelines until the day he died:

1. You cannot bring about prosperity by discouraging thrift.
2. You cannot help small men by tearing down big men.
3. You cannot strengthen the weak by weakening the strong.
4. You cannot lift the wage earner by pulling down the wage payer.
5. You cannot help the poor man by destroying the rich.
6. You cannot keep out of trouble by spending more than your income.
7. You cannot further the brotherhood of men by inciting class hatred.
8. You cannot establish security on borrowed money.
9. You cannot build character and courage by taking away man's initiative and independence.
10. You cannot help men permanently by doing for them what they could and should do for themselves.

Always be mindful that techniques and methods change, but principles never do. Therefore, the same principles that raised Andy from scarcity to abundance are capable of lifting you up to achieve even your fondest dreams. Herein, you have been given the secrets regarding how to build wealth. Learn them, believe them, live them, and you shall surely find the abundant life. No one is preventing you from achieving greatly but yourself. Take control of yourself, staying true to your calling, and one day the floodgates of prosperity will open wide and deluge you with *true* riches.

A wise man will place all his faith in his immutable maker for both prosperity and posterity.

X

—◆—

Opportunities many times
disguise themselves
as adversities.

—◆—

EPILOGUE

U nfortunately, the seven golden scrolls that were stolen from the museum of the International Society of Hebrew Studies in New York were never recovered. Captain Peter O'Day of the N.Y.P.D. said that the thieves probably melted them down and sold the gold for profit. His was most likely a good hypothesis since he was privy to the local underworld's rumor mill.

The irony of his hypothesis is most typical of human nature. The thieves, who were anxious to make a quick dollar, had in their possession the way to make millions and do it honestly. Instead, they destroyed their rare opportunity in exchange for no more than a few thousand dollars. How often men commit the same mistake in life through their pursuit of instant riches. Will they ever learn? Probably not, for this has been the situation throughout recorded history.

Andy held no ill will toward the International Society of Hebrew Studies, or its overseer, Rabbi Abraham Heschel. In his opinion, and rightly so, the real value of the seven golden scrolls was in their message. After all, they had guided him from poverty to great wealth. That was proof enough for a Scotsman. He said, "It is only in America that a man has the best opportunity to become the fruitful person that God intended him to be. But it is the responsibility of the man himself to take advantage of that opportunity."

The legend was born and kept alive through generations of the rabbinical order. The rabbi who told the story to me believed that the legend should now be made known to the world. His account of the tale was definitive and colorful. He alleged that the Andy of the legend was none other than the great Andrew Carnegie, the American steel magnate. At his insistence, I did some research on the life of Mr. Carnegie and must admit that his assertion could have credibility. I found certain incidents in the lives of the two men amazingly similar.

The legacy that remains, the message of the seven golden scrolls, is one of the most valuable gifts ever bequeathed to mankind, for it lights the way to the abundant life for anyone who dares to follow it. The secrets of building wealth are no longer hidden from the masses, but are openly revealed in the legacy. *True* riches cry out for just one person among the mass of humanity to hear the call and step forth and rise above every circumstance to become a mortal of uncommon destiny. My question to you is, are you that person?

BIBLIOGRAPHY

Bland, Glenn. *Success: The Glenn Bland Method*. Wheaton, IL: Tyndale House Publishers, Inc., 1972.

Carnegie, Andrew. *Autobiography of Andrew Carnegie*. Cambridge, MA: The Riverside Press, 1920.

Owen, G. Frederick. *Abraham Lincoln: The Man & His Faith*. Wheaton, IL: Tyndale House Publishers, Inc., 1976.

The Holy Bible, New International Version. New York: New York International Bible Society, 1978.

The Living Bible. Wheaton, IL: Tyndale House Publishers, 1971.

INDEX

Index

debt *(continued)*
    Tenet I, 82–83
    Tenet II, 83–87
    Tenet III, 87–88
    usury, 83
Demas, story of, 67–72
depreciation, 87
Divine Authority, 25
Divine bonding, 25
Divine order, 27, 43

E

Elymus, story of, 61–63
En-gedi wilderness, 13
estate planning, 74
extravagance, 84

F

Faith-Harvest, Miracle of,
        92–102
    First Law, 93–94
    Second Law, 94–96
    Third Law, 96–102
financial counsel, 35–38. *See also*
        financial plan
financial plan. *See also* financial
        counsel
    budgeting plan, 41–43
    Lesson One, 41–43
    Lesson Three, 44–45
    Lesson Two, 44
    Lesson Four, 45–49
    to restore credit, 86
free trade, establishment of, 110
free will, 24

G

get-rich-quick schemes, 36
giving, 91–97
    commitment to God, 92
goals, for building wealth
    Andy's example, 106–113
    list of, 45–49
    long- vs. short-range, 46–47
God's love, 15
gold. *See* Demas, story of

H

Hafid, story of, 37–38
happiness. *See* contentment
Hay, Secretary, 112
Heschel, Rabbi Abraham, 15, 117

I

industriousness, Andy's example,
        106–113
insurance, 67–75
intelligence, 24
International Society of Hebrew
        Studies, 14–15, 117
iron, the Civil War market for,
        109–110

J, K

Jesus, 5, 10
jiins, 5
John the Baptist, 10
Judean wilderness, 3, 13
King Saul, 13

Index

L

Law of Cause and Effect, 99–102
laziness. *See* slothfulness
leather cylinder, as artifact, 6
lending, 36
Lincoln, Abraham, 111–112
   his guidelines, 112
Lord, honoring the, 92
luck, 53
   belief in, as debilitating, 100

M

materialism, and fulfillment, 98
money
   attitude to, 26
   desire for, 28
   respect for, 28–29
multiplication of harvest, 56–58
Murabba'at, 3

N, O

naivety, 84
negative (destructive) emotions, 60
   fear, 14
   greed and envy, 26
O'Day, Captain Peter, 117

P, Q

parental influence, 84
patience, in obtaining results, 56
paying oneself, 34–35
perseverance, 58–59
poor, the, 94
pottery, as artifact, 5–6

prayer, 14
precepts, guiding, 44–45
Principles of the Harvest,
   53–59, 60
   Principle I, 54
   Principle II, 54–55
   Principle III, 55–56
   Principle IV, 56–57
   Principle V, 57–58
protection of wealth, 73. *See also*
   insurance
Psalm 37, 19
quality vs. quantity, 54
Qumran, 3

R

railway, as an example of expan-
   sion, 106–109
Reciprocity, Rule of, 61–62
respect of peers, 63
riches. *See* wealth
Rules of Financial Beginnings,
   33–38
   Rule 1, 33–34
   Rule II, 34–35
   Rule III, 35–38

S

sacrifice, 34
saving, 33–34
seed-giving, 95–96
self-discipline, 84
self-gratification, 84
service, providing to others, 59–64
   attributes to cultivate, 62

Index

About the Author

Glenn Bland began his career as a life insurance salesman for a large stock life insurance company in the early 1960s. After rising to the position of vice president of marketing, he decided to start his own national marketing company. The result was United Financial Network, a full-service financial services company, and one of the first of its kind. This company still flourishes today.

In addition to writing numerous industry publications, Mr. Bland is the author of *Success: The Glenn Bland Method,* a book that presents the basics of goal setting and planning. As a result of the success of this book, he has been asked to conduct numerous goal-setting seminars and has appeared on programs with such well-known motivational writers as Dr. Denis Wately, Og Mandino, and Zig Ziglar.

Recently Glenn Bland relinquished his day-to-day responsibilities as president and chief executive officer of United Financial Network to pursue a full-time writing career. He lives in Memphis, Tennessee, with his wife and children.